CODE NAME: BAKER CATCHER
The Human Side of World War II

Jack Ellis Westbrook

Erin Faith Allen
Zachariah Fike
and
Pathfinder Research LLC

Copyright © 2023 by **Jack Ellis Westbrook**

All rights reserved. No part of this publication may be reproduced, distributed or transmitted in any form or by any means, without prior written permission.

Jack Ellis Westbrook / Erin Faith Allen / Zachariah Fike / Pathfinder Research, LLC

Book Layout © 2014 BookDesignTemplates.com

Graphic Design: Michelle Tompkins
Cover Design: Erin Faith Allen

Editor: Celia Thrash / Erin Faith Allen / Zachariah Fike / Pathfinder Research LLC

Code Name: Baker Catcher
The Human Side of World War II
Jack Ellis Westbrook -- 1st ed.

Out of the four million fighting men who served during World War II, this is the story of one young man from a small Texas town of 3,000. He lived a simple life.
He worked in an icehouse or picked cotton during the summer, was captain of his six-man football team, and went to Texas A&M. He never thought twice about making sacrifices for his country or his family.
His story, told in his own words, celebrates his life and his journey during the War to End All Wars.

In dedication to our dad from his loving daughters,

        Cynthia Greer
        Cylvia Stevenson
        Celia Thrash

INTRODUCTION

For the past four or five years I have been accumulating material to put together an account of my Grandfather Westbrook's experiences in the Civil War. Just this past week, while visiting our daughter and telling her of my plans, she pointed out her interest in my own experiences in World War II. It had never occurred to me that our children would be curious since my experiences weren't unusual and actually pale in comparison to others. But with the seriousness of her request, I've written down some of my memories, hoping that they might provide my descendants what I would have liked them to have known about their Papa Jack. I hope you will enjoy it and that it will be meaningful to you. Keep in mind that it wasn't just me – there were sixteen million other young people. Consider that this was a window in history and that it may help put it all in perspective.

Maybe you'll go along with me if my memory isn't too accurate or complete – after all it has been over forty years since this writing and the military forbade us from keeping diaries. If captured, the diary with its daily entries would have breached security. But fortunately, time helps. It even makes us forget the more painful events and lets us enjoy the good and happy instances. You must understand why I don't tell all – there are some things that I am not proud of that would not serve the purpose intended in this book, and just as well should not be recorded. You'll probably guess that some events have been enhanced by having been repeated – or have neglected to have stayed fully refreshed in my memory. You'll only know what I want you to know; and I don't expect you to understand why.

As for not being able to remember all of my fellow GI's names, I apologize. It is a puzzle to me that I can't remember some of those friends who were so important to me, nor why I remember some over others. I know that after all of these years, I have such fond memories of the times I've had with them.

One of my greatest disappointments is that I haven't been able to let them know just how much I admire them, respect them, and thank them for being friends, acquaintances, fellow soldiers, team members, brave patriots – for making a cause the meaningful effort we made. I say this having viewed some of the criticism of the Korean and Vietnam efforts. We were indeed fortunate in that there was no question about the validity of the cause of that time. No one could mistake the seriousness or the hazard of the continuing issues with Japan, Italy, and Germany. We were united in our desire to stem the tides that threatened our country. We wanted to make a better world with a patriotic enthusiasm that was wonderful. We were young! War is a young person's responsibility with the stamina, dedication, adeptness, alertness, etc. that is required.

How fortunate I was to be privileged to live at that time, and that I was one of the more fortunate ones to come through relatively unscathed. I wouldn't take anything for having made the journey, wouldn't do it again for anything, and fervently pray that no one will ever have to make that extensive effort again. Don't misunderstand. I was hurt more than just a physical wound. I want to think that because of the course I followed after the war, I was able to overcome the psychological burden that I was left with. In this fact I am more than fortunate. My youth, my parents and brother, Skipper - my wife, and my three girls, all helped me to overcome some traumatic residues.

World War II was unique. Never before had a nation risen from the depths of a depression to build a war machine from scratch, equip its Allies, and coordinate its Allies on multiple world fronts to completely decimate two magnificent war machines. There may be more conventional wars in the future, but it is not likely. And if such should be our misfortune, it will in all probability be a limited nuclear conflict with much worse destruction and more casualties.

The likelihood of an all-out nuclear war is so probable that I won't allow myself to think about it. The fact that our homeland was not invaded or bombed in the last one hundred or more years may not be enjoyed in any future wars. Again, it is my prayer that our leaders can, and will, avoid any future wars. Our government and leaders toy with circumstances and situations which are so explosive that it is miraculous that we have escaped a nuclear war.

It is my hope that our children, grandchildren, and beyond will see in my account a boy, a young man, who was dedicated to his country and wanted desperately to do his part as a citizen and a patriot. I volunteered. I wasn't drafted and I did not shirk my duty. My contribution was not anything but ordinary, but only because that was all that was asked of me at the time. I'm proud of having fulfilled the opportunity that was offered me. I say that with a sincerity that only I know. If I have any gift to leave you, it will be this knowledge – along with whatever freedom may have come from my contribution.

With these matters under consideration, I will proceed with my account as it can be resurrected, trusting that any inaccuracies, errors in memory, and misstatements of fact will be overlooked and excused by those men who may have a better recollection. I have changed the names of some of the soldiers I name in the book; I don't want to sully their character through some of their actions during that time. Everyone's character was in question at some time or another during the war. That is what war does to a man. My intent is to tell the happenings just as they came about, not to leave out anything of importance, not to slight any one, and certainly not to paint a more glowing picture than events called for.

This is my story.

Jack E. Westbrook

AWARDS

First Lieutenant Jack E. Westbrook returned Stateside on June 8, 1946. He was placed in the Inactive Reserve on August 31, 1946. Lieutenant Westbrook received the following decorations and awards:

- **Bronze Star with one Oak Leaf Cluster and the V-Device**

- **Purple Heart**

- **Army Commendation Medal**

- **American Campaign Medal**

- **European-African-Middle Eastern Campaign Medal with two Campaign Stars (Rhineland and Central Europe)**

- **World War II Victory Medal**

- **Army of Occupation Medal (Germany Clasp)**

- **Combat Infantry Badge**

- **Médaille de la France Libérée**

CONTENTS

Introduction v
Awards ix
Preface 1

PART I: IN THE BEGINNING 3
    Chapter 1 - Becoming a Soldier 7
    Chapter 2 - Becoming an Officer 23
    Chapter 3 - Shipping Out 29

PART II: AT WAR 35
    Chapter 4 - Marseilles, France 37
    Chapter 5 - On to the Front 43
    Chapter 6 - The Last Straw 61
    Chapter 7 - Life at the Front 65
    Chapter 8 - Schweighausen, France 69
    Chapter 9 - Moyenvic, France 77
    Chapter 10 - Vosges Mountains, France 83
    Chapter 11 - Operation Undertone 91
    Chapter 12 - Returning to the Front 101

PART III: DACHAU 117
    Chapter 13 - Liberation of Dachau 119

PART IV: THE END OF THE WAR 133
    Chapter 14 - On to Munich 135
    Chapter 15 - On through Europe 139
    Chapter 16 - VE Day, Freutsmoos to Berchtesgaden ... 145

PART V: OCCUPATION 151
    Chapter 17 - Occupation by the US Forces in Austria 153
    Chapter 18 - Occupying Western Austria 165
    Chapter 19 - Vienna, Austria 177
    Chapter 20 - Assignment in Linz, Austria 191
    Chapter 21 - Deactivation of the Rainbow Division 201
    Chapter 22 - Fire Marshal of the US Forces in Austria 205

PART VI: GOING HOME 209
    Chapter 23 - The Final Goodbye 211
    Epilogue 215
    Afterword 219
    Acknowledgements 225

PREFACE

Did you know that mules scream when they're injured? It's a high-pitched, blood-curdling scream, almost like that of a mother who has lost her child. It's haunting and terrifying at the same time. This is the first thing I heard when I started to come to my senses. I heard our pack mules running and screaming, I heard the tat-tat-ta-tat-tat of machine guns, I heard muted yelling and the snap and crash of trees bursting. I smelled the acrid scent of smoke and that of the rotted leaves and icy dirt I lay on. As I slowly opened my eyes, I wasn't sure of what I was seeing. I saw smoke and haze, light falling snow, and the trees above me were gnarled and cut into odd shapes from direct hits. Can I move? With effort, I tried to move up on elbows, but fell back down to the ground. Was I injured or just knocked out? I wasn't in pain; I just couldn't move. As I darted my eyes from side to side trying to glimpse some remembrance of where I was, I tried to shake my foggy mind and understand details of what had happened. How did a poor twenty year old boy from a small west Texas town end up all alone, lying wounded on the floor of a forest in Germany? It was in those moments that I began to remember.

I remembered the past, not too long ago, and that sunny day where it all began....

PART I: IN THE BEGINNING

"We interrupt this broadcast to bring you this important bulletin from the United Press.
FLASH!
The White House announces Japanese attack on Pearl Harbor. Stay tuned to W.O.R. for further developments. Which will be broadcast immediately as received."

CHAPTER ONE

BECOMING A SOLDIER
A&M COLLEGE OF TEXAS
ROOM 411, DORMITORY 5
DECEMBER 7, 1941
2:00 PM

I joined the Reserve Officers Training Corps (ROTC) at A&M College (it wasn't renamed A&M University until 1963) in 1941 and shared the cadet residence with the other members of the Corps. I was in Room 411, Dormitory 5 on the A&M campus, studying my freshman engineering courses on a quiet Sunday afternoon when I heard the announcement. Most of the students in the all-male dorm rooms were glued to their radios listening to the New York Giants and the Brooklyn Dodgers* football game when I heard a loud chorus of groans and shouts emitting from other rooms on my floor. The noise was widespread. There wasn't air conditioning in the dorm rooms back then so all of the windows were open. From window to window, a scattering of radio alerts could be heard from all different directions as we heard the chilling report of the Japanese attack on Pearl Harbor. Only the privileged students had radios, so for the rest of us, we ran to our windows, stuck out our heads, and quieted to hear any information we could.

---

*The Brooklyn Dodgers was an American football team that played in the NFL from 1930-1943. In 1944, their name was changed to the Brooklyn Tigers.

> *"Hello, Hello, NBC. This is KTU in Honolulu, Hawaii.... I am speaking from the roof of the Advertiser Publishing Company Building. We have witnessed this morning the distant view, a brief, full battle of Pearl Harbor and the severe bombing of Pearl Harbor by enemy planes, undoubtedly Japanese. The city of Honolulu has also been attacked and considerable damage done. This battle has been going on for nearly three hours. One of the bombs dropped within fifty feet of KTU tower. It is no joke. It is a real war. The public of Honolulu has been advised to keep in their homes and away from the Army and Navy. There has been serious fighting going on in the air and in the sea. The heavy shooting seems to be ... (interruption) We cannot estimate just how much damage has been done, but it has been a very severe attack. The Navy and Army appear now to have the air and the sea under control."**

After hearing the stark news, most of the cadets rushed to the halls to get on phone lines to call family, girlfriends, or anyone they could to rehash those moments and what it would mean to their future. The news of the attack had strong consequences for all of us, especially the ROTC students, myself included. To some it was disbelief, shock or surprise, but to others it was a relief. Finally we knew the course our country would take. The US would go to war. During the past few years our country kept its distance from world events: Germany was at war with England; Russia was a menace; France had fallen; Poland had been decimated; and Italy created its own part of the debacle. Now it all came to the forefront. No doubt each of us had an idea of what the moment meant to us as individuals, and we all had our own premonitions of what lay ahead of us.

Many Aggies left school that day, preparing to answer the call that inevitably would be issued. Others, at the request from school advisors and government officials, opted to remain in class and continue their education for the immediate future. This was the course I took. As

---

*The above quote is the actual copy of the live announcement made from KTU Broadcasting in Honolulu, Hawaii.

the days went by with the continuous reports of our country gearing up its war machine, those of us staying behind became restless and found it difficult to concentrate on studies. We constantly questioned ourselves on whether we should drop out of school and go on to war or stay as we had been advised. My parents encouraged me to stay in school, stating it was the best way to immediately serve my country. Still, good judgment aside, I was torn with the feeling that my country needed me and I didn't want to hide behind anything. It was a traumatic battle I fought within myself on a daily basis.

It didn't take long before Texas A&M College became full-on military. In addition to the physical training and educating of the student body, the ROTC took on the technical training of several hundred servicemen on campus. It was an all-out effort. Our future in the military became more probable and our excitement grew when new and more sophisticated equipment came in for our training as well as new military personnel being added to the teaching staff. Quickly our semesters were shortened and our studies and military training were sped up. By December 12, 1942 the entire Texas A&M Corps of cadets was inducted into the Enlisted Reserve. In that same month, at the age of eighteen years, I contracted with the Army to receive a commission as a Second Lieutenant, Infantry, upon my successful completion of Advanced Reserve Officers Training. The wheels of war were turning and now I stood in its direct path.

There was no turning back.

CAMP WOLTERS

It was only a few months later, on March 23, 1943 that the entire ROTC status as Enlisted Reservists at A&M was changed to Active and we were shipped to Camp Wolters, near Mineral Wells, Texas. Coming in as privates, we would be paid $30 per month and given a full issue of government clothing and equipment. What a disappointment to have to give up our quasi-officers uniforms we had worn at school! We thought we had already been trained enough to come in as commissioned officers, but for obvious reasons including our age, maturity and inexperience, we were leveled to the lowly private class. What a pity! At the time, we didn't understand nor appreciate the "why". In fact, we were haughty enough to believe the Army had betrayed us.

Because we hadn't completed the final year of our Advanced ROTC contract at school before being shipped out, the Army placed my group (class of 1945) in basic training until there was an opening in Officer Candidate School (OCS) – our ultimate goal. Again, we didn't like this at all. It seemed that we were starting all over again, but we were "in the Army" now and had to adhere to their rules. Because we had some status in the Corps, several of my fellow cadets and I decided to transfer to the Tank Destroyer Force, where there was a promise we could gain a quicker entry into OCS. As a group, we were determined to become officers as soon as possible and by whatever means we could. We put our papers in for the transfer and once again packed our bags and loaded onto the bus for our next location.

NORTH CAMP HOOD

The tank destroyer training base was at North Camp Hood (now Fort Hood) located near Killeen, Texas. The north camp was an addition to the main camp and still under construction, so it was primitive to say the least. Enthusiastic as we were, when we got off the bus and looked at our surroundings, we felt the first pang of what our lives were about to become. The barracks were one-story, tar-paper covered huts in a bleak, almost desert-like terrain. It was hot, and there were no latrines, which meant we straddled trenches. We used portable showers and didn't have any electricity.

Thankfully, these conditions were only temporary and would soon change, but what didn't change is my fellow Aggies and I (there were eight of us) were the only Aggies in the two hundred and fifty man training company. The other soldiers were from California and Arizona, and were less fortunate and lacked good education and proper training compared to the seasoned Aggies. But now we were all on the same level, and to make it through this we had to work together. In hindsight, it turned out to be excellent training. Our entire career in the military up to this point had been with classmates from A&M who were for the most part, our equals. Now we were training with men who hadn't the education or physical discipline we were accustomed to. As future officers, we needed to understand how the general population would perform on a battlefield and our time here opened our eyes and gave us plenty of insight.

The Tank Destroyer Force had one of the highest morales of all the Army units. Maybe this was because of the toughness in our training procedures. One might say it was close to that of the Marine Corps which had always been known for its brutal training. Yet as hard as the training was, it only solidified our determination. The non-commissioned officers who supervised our training were merciless on us from 3:30 am until lights out at 9:30 pm. As Aggies, and the status of our school being considered a class above the rest of the colleges, we were targeted and given more responsibilities. We were constantly reminded that as leaders we would have to work harder in our position as role models. And we did.

Inspections were easy for the eight of us. We had learned the routine early on while at A&M. But the other recruits, in general, were slovenly and had to learn a few hard lessons. The extreme heat, the crude conditions at the camp, and some unusually strict rules made the thirteen weeks we had to endure a nightmare. But in the end, it was the routine physical training that tested our limits. It wasn't unusual for us to run an infiltration course with live machine guns firing overhead and charges blowing up around us as we crawled three hundred feet on our bellies under barbed wire entanglements with full field packs on our back.

During our training period, it was the equipment that fascinated us. One of my favorites was learning to handle the M3 half-track with its .50 caliber machine guns. The half-track is an armored military vehicle designed to carry personnel or equipment through rough ground or open warfare. It has wheels in the front and tracks in the back and could scramble through almost any kind of terrain. It was well-known to carry generals to the front lines or transport injured soldiers to safety.

The most popular weapon we would be using is one which usually shows up in photos and videos of wartime in Europe - the 57mm Anti-Tank Gun.

Large and mounted on rubber tires, it was highly mobile and was usually towed behind half-tracks or military tractors. They were powerful weapons with a high muzzle velocity and armor piercing capabilities. Even with its minimal sight functioning, it was still useful against lighter tanks, half-tracks, armored artillery, and numerous other targets. Because the gun's characteristic blast identifies its location to the enemy, our tactics would call for two quick rounds to be fired from a gun position, then men had to hurriedly relocate the gun before its position could be zeroed in on by the enemy. This required several men to move the gun quickly and efficiently using lots of muscle and coordination with no room for error or lagging. We became well-trained in this maneuver and would soon find it to be one of our most effective forces.

Another favorite was the M3 mounted with 75mm cannons. As a group we loved training on these monsters. We were like kids with a big, new toy.

As time passed, I not only learned schedules and routines, but even more important, I learned the different temperaments of our commanders and their feelings towards their wards. It was disturbing to witness some of the vicious events that occurred. Segregation in the Army was in full force. African Americans were allowed to serve, but they were still subjected to mistreatment and discrimination which was hard for us to watch. The black soldiers had to face racial segregation in the town of Killeen as well. We were angry but as privates there was little we could do or say without dire consequences.

There was a particularly nasty corporal, Corporal Steele, a name indelible in every cadet's memories. For some reason, he harbored a particular resentment for the Aggies, and he seemed to enjoy reminding us of our lowly position. One of his favorite disciplinary moves was to put boxing gloves on men and encourage them to take their aggression out on each other through an unofficial boxing match - just "to take the sap out of them". On one such occasion Steele gathered us into a barren bunkhouse where he pitted one of my fellow Aggies against a big Arizona Native American twice his size. It was clear that Steele was looking forward to making a point with us. As we gathered in a circle around the two mismatched opponents, one look would make you think this crazy exercise of Steele's would be over in a blink; however, the Native American soon learned that his adversary had been an intramural boxing champion and their match was over in minutes with the Aggie as the victor. As joyous as we were over the win, it only made Steele's resentment against us grow as he angrily marched out of the building without saying a word. In spite of our trying to be friends with him and the other trainees, officers, and noncoms, we were never able to establish friendships.

Officers could make our life in the barracks just as difficult. When a soldier was sloppy with his equipment, it was hell to pay for everyone in his unit when his commander discovered the mess. The entire unit would suffer for his blunder and we would have to stay up all night doing sit-ups, cleaning latrines, and other insufferable punishments. Although we weren't commanders nor angels, when we were pushed, we had our own system of teaching the lessons of the barracks, and we managed to correct the situation the GI way. One day a soldier secretly put heavy rocks in the duffle bag of one of the more untidy trainees who had given us plenty of grief with our commander. He carried them on two maneuvers before finding the excess weight. Quietly and quickly, he learned to clean out his duffle bags before future maneuvers! Other lessons were better learned on our own. One day I personally learned to never chew tobacco on the firing range in one hundred and five degree weather. Targets wouldn't stay still and I vomited every time I stood up.

Desert training was the main thrust or focus for us due to the lessons being learned in the African Campaign. Despite the heat, all of our movements were in the form of double-times where we would fast-pace our marching to one hundred and eighty steps-per-minute with a thirty-inch stride. The days were exhausting and the heat was scorching. Coming into camp in the evening from a full day of field training, we were required to have just enough water left in our canteen from our one-quart daily ration to take a number of salt tablets. These were given freely to soldiers as a supplement when sodium levels were suspected to be dipping dangerously low due to the heavy perspiration. The tablets were common then to help soldiers retain hydration and keep their electrolytes balanced so we took them without question. I recall all of the salt tablets we took back then when I hear today of the damage they can cause to your health. One thing was certain, the soldiers would not have made it through training without supplemental salt. Several tried to skip the salt tablets only to suffer the next day with cramps and nausea from the dehydration.

There was little relief from the rigorous training and the watchful eye of our trainers - not to mention the inferno heat of our crude barracks life, but off-duty we had the Post Exchange (PX) and Service Club to give us some respite. The Postal Exchange was a shop where we could spend our money on writing materials, snacks, and personal items but the most popular spot was the Service Club. Here a group of us would gather, get a beer or two, relax, and grumble about the day. We let out a lot of steam during those times and became the best of friends.

Four days before our basic training experience at North Camp Hood was to come to an end, an announcement was made that the Tank-Destroyers OCS had been closed. What a disappointment!

We felt sure we were going straight to school and on to becoming officers. The news deflated our spirits terribly and as fate would have it, we heard another bitter announcement: there wasn't room for us at Infantry OCS at Fort Benning, Georgia, either. We had played our cards wrong, and now we were left with nowhere to go but back to school.

Even though we were now reclassified as Army Specialized Trainees, we left the camp with our heads down and dolefully returned to Texas A&M to resume our studies once again. After the disappointment, our mental attitude on campus just wasn't the same. It was difficult to settle down to serious studies in light of what we had been through, and now we had to just sit and watch as the world events escalated. Our military supervisors understood our feelings and called on us to make the best of it, knowing that in time we would become officers. As it turned out, the delay could have been our salvation. We learned that one of the cadets from our group of Aggies dropped out of school and was sent directly overseas and killed in action. This was terrible news for us; we had become friends during our trials at Camp Hood.

Now we were seven.

After completing another mini-semester at school, the day came when we were transferred to Fort McClellan near Anniston, Alabama to enter yet another basic training. This time we were assigned to infantry status where we would remain. We were excited and eager for the transfer when we boarded a troop train to take us from College Station to Alabama. As luck would have it, I was assigned to Kitchen Patrol (KP) duty. I sat on a stool and peeled potatoes the entire trip. To make matters worse, our train to Alabama was extended several days by deviating routes across the country, to confuse the enemy of our plans. As we came to know, Germany was constantly spying on the US and its activities – even the training programs. We were the pawns in the game of confusing the enemy.

FORT MCCLELLAN

We arrived at Fort McClellan, Alabama on October 2, 1943 and the seven of us found ourselves back with many of our old classmates to begin yet another basic training course. Several of the other ROTC students that were gathering at Fort McClellan came from schools similar in status to A&M such as The Citadel - the military school located in South Carolina, Georgia Tech, and other fine institutions. Our group of seven was a bit more unusual in that we had gone through additional training in both ROTC and Tank Destroyer basics.

With all of its grass, water, and trees, Fort McClellan was the Garden of Eden when compared to North Camp Hood. The facility, being a permanent fort, provided a more adequate and full facility for our training. Here, once again, we found that as Aggies we were shown special consideration and given additional responsibilities as squad leaders and training assistants. But what worked even more to our advantage was that our company commander, Captain Anderson, seemed to like us. And we liked him.

Meanwhile, our new-found camaraderie with fellows of like background, social levels, and ideals made the training period more bearable, and even enjoyable. There was lots of good fun mixed in with the seriousness. On one occasion when a group of us were on KP duty, we learned to love the taste of honeydew melons. We had to have more! One night, while unloading supplies from an incoming truck, we found the crate of melons and secretly rolled a number of them under the mess hall as we entered the delivery door. Later that evening, after the kitchen had closed and the lights were out, we crawled on our stomachs under the mess hall building, and took them back to the barracks for a feast!

Not all of our antics were fun, and many of them I'd rather forget. I remember "Odom the Odor." Odom was a young recruit who was possibly even more "country" than I was. I think he was from Kentucky. During our time at Fort McClellan, it became evident that Odom didn't take a shower every day or maybe not at all during the week. Understand that after a full sixteen hours a day of sweating through the rigorous exercises and the grueling marches through the muck, we smelled pretty ugly. This didn't set well with the fellows sharing a barracks with him. After a couple of weeks, a group of cadets decided to give Odom a "GI Bath." Now, a GI Bath is about as cruel a lesson as can be forced upon a man. It involves using a stiff bristle brush to clean the dirty victim. Pretty soon, during the bath, the bristles begin to eat into the flesh, sometimes to the point of the flesh bleeding. Imagine five or six guys converging on a fellow cadet, forcing him into the shower (sometimes with his clothes on) giving him a treatment with the stiff bristled brush loaded down with lye soap! I never was part of those "GI baths," and it was hard to hear Odom's whimpering and at times, crying. He was a sensitive person, which made his treatment seem even crueler. However, once he had his bath, they never had to do it again. I can't say that I'm proud of some of the shenanigans that took place. But, that was how it was in the barracks.

Infantry basic training was fairly simple with conditioning and preparation. The group of us sailed through with high ratings and received excellent recommendations from our tactical officers. Surely, we hoped, this time we could go on to OCS at Fort Benning.

We couldn't believe it, but it wasn't to be! Although we were accepted and ready to go on to OCS, there wasn't availability. The OCS was filled up again! On January 5, 1944, we once again returned to A&M, discouraged and angry. I went on to complete another mini-semester and was classified as a senior in electrical engineering. When we really thought about it, staying on campus wasn't exactly bad duty. The dormitories and campus life certainly beat the military barracks. Fortunately, the accelerated study programs kept our noses to the grindstones; however, the general atmosphere on campus was less like college than it had ever been.

Finally, at the end of the mini-semester on March 10th, 1944 we received orders to go to Fort Benning's OCS. This was the moment we had been waiting for! We whooped and hollered as we packed our bags for OCS - this time knowing it would be our last.

ON TO FORT BENNING AND OFFICERS CANDIDATE SCHOOL

We loaded a troop train from College Station to Georgia via New Orleans. This time I didn't have KP duty and the Pullman cars were a pleasant change from my previous troop train experience. At New Orleans the train stopped for a time and many of us took a little too much liberty in seeing the neighborhood in which we found ourselves. Even though we were soldiers, we were still relatively young kids, so we tended to stretch the bounds of discipline.

One of the GIs shared with us that Sophie Newcomb College, the women's College of Tulane University, was nearby. It didn't take long for us to find the directions of the college and march to our destination. When the young women looked out their dorm room windows and saw handsome soldiers coming down the street, they were more than happy to yell and wave at us to get our attention. They playfully invited us to their windows for a visit and we were happy to accommodate. A few girls snuck out of their windows and ran to greet us while others blew kisses, encouraging us even more! In that relatively short time, we made life miserable for the dorm mothers. When the train sounded its whistle to warn of its departure, many of the men, who wanted to stay for one last smile, found themselves running behind the train, and grabbing at the rails to jump on as it took off - inevitably without some of them. Our officers considered disciplining those that didn't make it, but the charges were dropped because of the sheer number of soldiers involved!

After the train ride and a brief bus ride, we stepped into Fort Benning. From that moment on, we knew we were in a new class of competition. There was no question that our ROTC training and previous basic trainings put us in an excellent position; however, the pressure of being observed and graded twenty four hours a day was a nerve-wracking experience for all of us. Since there was a surplus of available officers at the time with only a few spots to fill, we found ourselves in stiff competition. We had been told that only twenty five percent of the company would graduate and the rules were inflexible. Anything from failing the academics, the physical evaluation, or the "failure to adapt" could get a cadet eliminated from the course.

Our tactical officers demanded both physical and mental stamina from each of us and our days quickly filled with extensive drills, calisthenics, marches, and learning how to bivouac - a sort of camp without tents or cover. The worst part of our training was being constantly scrutinized under observant and critical eyes. As nineteen and twenty year olds we were up to the physical and mental exercises, but the pressure of the scrutiny took us to another level. In-class studies and group training sessions were particularly taxing as well. If we failed to provide textbook solutions or if we gave a wrong answer, we were to receive severe penalties and demerits and no one wanted to risk failing.

On bivouacs or on the training fields, where time was in short supply, we were expected to keep our gear impeccable - rain or shine. Individual rifles had to pass rigid inspections at any moment. Our equipment had to be clean, orderly and stowed in the proper GI manner, and there would be no exceptions, even in inclement weather. There was some competition among candidates, but mostly we competed with ourselves and for our tactical officers.

An important element of our training was to orient us on the history of the war and why it was being fought. There were numerous lectures on the politics involved: the German, Italian, and Japanese threats to take over the world, the use of slave labor by the Axis Powers (there wasn't mention of the concentration camps or Jewish discrimination), along with the historical development of countries. This seemed unnecessary because we were already enthusiastic to put a stop to the threat against our country and we didn't need any coaching to tell us why we would be fighting. Probably the most impressive parts of these orientations were the first-hand accounts of combat by veteran officers. Their stories of the battlefield helped indoctrinate us as future officers to train and lead the soldiers under our command. While one officer would focus on navigating the difficult terrain and weather, another would tell the tales of the cruelty the German soldier was happy to inflict.

We studied virtually every aspect of any situation in which the infantry officer could be expected to find himself in: tactical problems involving artillery, air cover, engineer units, tanks, tank destroyers, chemical units, and paratroopers. A variety of realistic situations on the battlefield were reenacted in field maneuvers where each candidate was given a chance to demonstrate how he would conduct his unit in that scenario. He was placed in a position of either a platoon leader, company commander, forward observer, or staff officer. We also learned how to employ troops, handle live explosives, and the use of a variety of different types of equipment. Unlike the movies, all of these components added to the utter confusion of combat situations. Most of the uncertainty for us as leaders was when the pseudo-enemy forces changed their attack or defensive positions at a moment's notice, leaving us to quickly adjust our plans on the spot. Purposefully, our tactical officers would inject a maximum amount of chaos into the problem, making it practically impossible for any one of us to function satisfactorily in the eyes of our critics. He would have to perform his duties while being observed and graded by critical tactical officers. Many broke under the pressure, walking away from the situation completely devastated. What a disservice to our country! And yet, the situations we faced in training were closer to reality than we would have known at the time; and in just a few more months we would recognize the similarities.

Our tactical officers did a masterful job considering the short time they had to train young boys to become young officers. This wasn't a personality contest nor was politics of much importance. In the final analysis it was what the individual candidate could produce, gauged by extremely high standards, that led to his commission.

During the five month training period at Fort Benning, only two passes were given to the candidates. Most of us turned our passes back in so that we could stay on post to study or collapse with exhaustion. One weekend, some buddies and I regretfully took a pass to a town near Columbus. Unfortunately, the bars were all too eager to take a young soldier's money. Feeling broke and totally discouraged, we ended up coming back to our barracks early to rest and study. From that point on, we seldom took the opportunity to even go to the PX or a movie! The only real breather we received was attending church each Sunday, but even then it wasn't uncommon to see one of us nod off to sleep.

Towards the final days at the camp, each of us was subject to an intensive interview with our tactical officer. We were assigned to a small room with only a desk and two chairs where we would sit directly across from the officer. In the beginning of the interview, the officer would be friendly with light conversation, and slowly the interview would turn stern, then demanding, then ultimately it would become degrading and harsh. The objective of the interview was to assess the candidate's ability to respond under pressure. I was fortunate to have Lieutenant Foster leading my interview. Although he had to follow certain procedures that were set, he never let an interview end without showing a concern for the candidate's well-being.

What seemed to be a never-ending life of training finally came to an end. This phase of my journey was one of the most stringent and most indelible chapters in my life. We didn't know until we were formally presented the scroll, whether we were actually going to receive our commission. There were two hundred candidates in the company in the beginning. However, only ninety two finished the course to become officers.

As happy as we were to know we were going to become officers, we were disillusioned to hear the outcome for others. It was commonly known among us at the time that one of the candidates who had previously been eliminated was a young Jewish boy kicked out because an influential non-commissioned officer didn't like Jews. The candidate was of Lebanese origin and one of the nicest, most intelligent, and enthusiastic candidates in the company. He had all the characteristics of being a good officer. Since he was a good friend and fellow Aggie of mine, it was disappointing to later hear he had been sent to the front lines fourteen days after being kicked out and was eventually killed in the invasion of Normandy. A tragic end, and just one of many which I would come to know.

With this behind us we realized that the dream we all had from our freshman year was finally a reality. At nineteen years old, I was now a 2nd Lieutenant! Sadly, there wasn't anyone around to tell about our exuberance. No parents, wives, or siblings could be at the official ceremony. We received our diploma with only empty seats to look at.

Once we received our commission, our next concern was to wonder what our assignment would be. Was it to be a replacement in the front lines of a combat zone? Were we to lead a squad at a training camp? Were we to train more troops here in the US? I received my orders and couldn't have been happier to discover I was one of the lucky ones and had been assigned to the Anti-Tank Company, 222nd Infantry Regiment, 42nd Infantry "Rainbow" Division. Being part of the 42nd Division was an honor for any soldier. Its name alone was famously known during WWI when Douglas MacArthur said they would "stretch over the country like a rainbow." Next, I would be sent to Camp Gruber near Muskogee, Oklahoma to meet my squads and to receive further orders.

CHAPTER TWO

BECOMING AN OFFICER
CAMP GRUBER
JUNE 20TH, 1944

After a one week leave at home, I reported to Camp Gruber and to Colonel Henry Luongo, my Regimental Commander. Camp Gruber was located in the Cookson Hills at the foothills of Oklahoma's Ozark Mountains. It was a beautiful area compared to the dusty and barren west Texas home I came from, but it had eighty seven square miles of harsh terrain combed over with grass, trees and water. It was a perfect setting for new troops to train. Maneuvering over the terrain would be rough, arduous, and yet as we came to know, eerily realistic for what was in store for our division once we faced our future battlegrounds.

Luongo gave me my assignment to an Anti-Tank company because of my experience in Tank Destroyer training. It was a choice assignment in an infantry unit, and I was pleased that my Camp Hood experience hadn't entirely been in vain. There was a short orientation concerning Camp Gruber and the Rainbow Division, where afterwards I was able to become acquainted with regimental commanders and a few other top brass.

Finally, the time came for my assignment to BOQ (Bachelor Officers Quarters) with the man who was to be an inspiration to me – Captain Mike Tursi, my company commander. Tursi was a twenty eight year old, 5'2" Greek with ego and gutsiness personified! He had a strong personality and was self-confident with intelligence and experience to back it up. From the moment we met there was no doubt as to who was in command – it was a good start for a shaky young officer. After our introductions, I couldn't wait to get to my barrack and start my new job of leading my men. I was just out of OCS - a green, idealistic, 2nd Lieutenant - leader of the 2nd Platoon with three squads containing nine-twelve men each. I was in charge now and I thought I could rule the world.

Eager to meet my men, Tursi and I burst through the doors of the 2nd Platoon barracks. There, lying on a bunk with his arms behind his head and legs crossed nonchalantly was the infallible platoon sergeant Geary, looking cocky and smug as he quipped, "What's up Sir?" Deflated from the less-than-respectful greeting, I stammered up to meet the first of one of my men.

Geary was regular Army, about twenty eight years old, 5'10", very thin at about 150lbs, slightly stooped, and about as unmilitary a figure as you can imagine. He was assigned as the platoon sergeant directly under my lead. I have to say that despite that first impression of him, he was later to become, in my eyes, the epitome of what an excellent Non-Commissioned Officer (NCO) should be. He had the capability of getting more out of the men while lying on his bunk than any lieutenant could by running all over the platoon and company areas! He commanded the respect of his men, his fellow NCOs, and officers of the regiment. His influence was critical in the training and maintaining of discipline of the platoon – all while maintaining a low profile. Best of all, he had the unique ability to run the platoon yet allow me to think I was.

After that first brief moment with Geary, I regained my composure and went on to meet my squad leaders, radio men, jeep driver, and the men of the first, second, and third squads. All of the men were green but seemed receptive to being molded into my idea of a first class unit. Most of the men had come from an Army Specialized Training Program (ASTP) and were young, sharp, and willing to work. Commanding these men was as natural as breathing to me, and once again, thanks to Geary, I was able to fulfill my duties.

A/T COMPANY COMPOSITION

The A/T company (short for Anti-Tank) in an infantry regiment was composed of three gun platoons, a mine platoon, and a headquarters section. Headquarters section consisted of the company commander, executive officer, reconnaissance officer, first sergeant, the administrative group, and motor pool. The company commander had the overall command of the company with its duties and responsibilities. The executive officer, in addition to being second in command, had the responsibilities of administration, supplies, and the motor pool.

The gun platoons were composed of three squads, with each having one 57mm Anti-Tank Gun. The platoon leader was a second lieutenant, the platoon sergeant was a technical sergeant, and each squad leader was a staff sergeant. Gunners were buck sergeants, and assistant gunners were corporals as were the vehicle drivers. There were nine to twelve men in a squad. The platoon leader had a jeep with a driver who was also a radio operator and runner. The mine platoon had the same organization except there were four squads specializing in the use of anti-tank and anti-personnel mines.

Within our regimental area, the A/T Company had its own designated living areas which had four barracks, a supply room, and a headquarters with a day room attached. During stateside training, all of our vehicles were kept in a regimental motor pool as a matter of efficiency.

TRAINING AT CAMP GRUBER

At the beginning of training, my first order of business was to see that my men were in top physical condition. Our day began at 4:00 am and ended at 10:00 pm seven days a week. In the middle of the hot summer, we began with physical training and ended with long and demanding drills intended to shape us into a sharp and disciplined unit. Ongoing gun drills, twenty five mile hikes under full field pack (and some double timing), incessant studying of equipment, merciless inspections, rifle range and gunnery range practice, and tactical maneuvers were all designed to keep us in shape and fine-tune our abilities as well as temper the pride of the soldiers.

Division problems were always being discussed with our supporting units - those of artillery, air, engineers, and chemical units. With this being said, our biggest challenge was learning to adapt to field exercises through the chaos of simulated warfare. Our major goal was to successfully coordinate and communicate with adjacent and supporting units. It was a bigger job than I would have expected.

Our normal functions in the field were never a problem until it was disrupted by other wandering units passing through on their own field trials. Then, we'd have to rethink our exercises and adapt to the new situation. This happened over and over again.

On the lighter side of the challenges I had to contend with, one seemed unsolvable - watermelons! I couldn't keep the GIs out of the local melon patches. Some poor soul at headquarters had his work cut out for him paying the local natives for their missing melons. Somehow, soldiers couldn't comprehend the necessity of their staying out of the melon patches and we dealt with the issue throughout our time at Camp Gruber giving out demerits and punishing exercises, but it did little good.

After four months of training, the men were given some Sundays off and an occasional Saturday afternoon pass. Headquarters wasn't giving out many official leaves and then they were only allowed for emergency purposes. When these were given out, headquarters only gave them to a small part of the unit at a time so that training could continue with little or no interruption. As the weeks passed and our training progressed, there was no doubt in our minds of the seriousness of the work we were doing and that our time was closing in. It was only a question of "when" we would be shipped out and "where" we would go.

AN EMBARRASSING STRAIN

The toll of training caught up with me in August of 1944. The punishing physical training, double-timing, heavy work combined with the long hours riding in tank destroyers and in the back of trucks caused me to be afflicted with hemorrhoids to the extent I was incapacitated! This led to corrective surgery, the description and effect of which is best not spelled out on these pages. It was probably the severest test of my life - drastically debilitating. While my hospital stay was short, it was two long months before I was able to enter into the training regimen fully, and two long months of constant banter from my fellow soldiers of my most embarrassing situation!

A COLORFUL DIVISION

Our training continued, and as it did, our morale soared as we became a first class fighting machine. One of my gun squads was recognized by the regimental and division commanders for our excellence in training accomplishments. From time to time, some of the men were pulled out and sent overseas as replacements, but for the most part, my company remained intact. I was disappointed to say goodbye to my initial company commander, but the division received an outstanding new officer in Major General Harry Collins who was now to lead the 42nd 'Rainbow' Infantry Division.

Collins, in his wisdom, chose to make our division as colorful as its name indicated; and, as a result of the color and flourish, it became known as "Hollywood Harry's" division. This was an important accomplishment because his strive for high morale was working. We were proud to be in the Army and we were exuberant over the Rainbow designation we could claim. Scattered within our training and giving us a little reprieve, were several festive division parades which touted the motto, "Never Forget", and our new division song, "That Good Ole Mountain Dew" (a take-off from Camp Gruber being located in the Cookson Hills of Oklahoma). It was played as a march and it stirred the cockles of the GI's hearts. The display of the

Rainbow and its colors in the company areas, the frequent pep-talks (many by Collins himself) and the use of bright blue scarves with our tunics to match our Rainbow patches made for an exhilarating time during a serious situation.

CHAPTER THREE

SHIPPING OUT
NOVEMBER, 1944

During the early fall, it became clear to us that our division was preparing for overseas shipment. Equipment was replenished and conditioned, manpower was brought to full strength, and our clothing and personal equipment were brought up to standards. Headquarters held orientations for the troops to help them finalize their affairs and those families that were living on base were sent home. The air was changing and it was easy to see our time was coming soon. One of our last tasks, which was a job we hated, was to prepare our equipment with cosmoline. Cosmoline is a wax-like corrosion inhibitor. All of our equipment and guns, even entire tanks and guns had to be greased with it before shipping out to prepare them for the corrosion that would undoubtedly occur on the ocean voyage. After wiping everything down with that awful stuff, we then had to crate and ship out all of the equipment. Although there was every indication that the appointed time was near, we were still not given any hint as to where or when the division would be sent. Our excitement was only from the ever-present anticipation of what lay ahead. The tone in the camp changed considerably from the serious to the very serious.

The day of shipping out finally arrived on November 12, 1944. All troops boarded a train at Braggs, Oklahoma - the nearest rail siding from Camp Gruber. It was an orderly, quiet, and almost solemn operation as the men, one by one, stepped onto the train and took their seat as each train car moved slowly out of the siding and headed north. Not knowing where we were headed and what our fate would be was a constant topic of conversation in the hours and days of traveling.

This trip was better for me. As an officer I had all kinds of allowances, I even had a berth on a Pullman car. What a luxury! As much as I enjoyed the privileges that came with being an officer, I felt a twinge of guilt knowing that my men were not being cared for equally as well. During our journey, there was some attempt at training but it wasn't successful at all. It was difficult to organize guard duty and to keep troops from wandering off while the trains stopped for supplies. Excitement was too high, and young minds just couldn't follow the gist of the work. No amount of discipline could have mustered success in any training program at this point. Most of the men played poker or read. As officers, we kept constant contact with our men. We would walk up and down the aisles of the train and at random times would check out their berths. Gratefully, my company kept intact and out of trouble during the entire trip.

With two hundred and nineteen men cooped up on a train, difficulties were bound to spring up. We had problems with the sick, problems for the men at home, and other minor disciplinary infractions. This many men cooped up on a small train for such an extended time led to temper flare-ups and unruly disagreements. At times we even had problems with the recreational activities. There was a never-ending demand of our time as administrators. Sometimes it seemed that administration was the biggest factor in running an Army.

Once we arrived in Chicago, the train detoured and headed east which we grasped to mean "to Europe". However, we were told by the Transportation Corps personnel that troops headed for the Pacific left eastern ports as well. Here again, we were confused as to where we would be sent. After three days on the train, shuttled from one direction to another (all to deceive the enemy) we arrived at Camp Kilmer, New Jersey. From here, we were to be transported to the port of New York City and to embark on a ship to take us to God-knows-where.

We arrived at camp ahead of our equipment. Apparently, there was a two to three day delay in it being shipped - not an unusual occurrence in the Army. It was a nuisance for us to have to wait, but it gave us the opportunity to receive a few days of leave so we could get one last taste of our homeland.

Several of us made the trip to New York City where we undoubtedly overdid the drinking and carousing. But, for the most part, those days remain a special memory. I remember the glamorous Commodore Hotel on 42nd Street and Lexington with its grand chandeliers and plush carpet and another favorite hang-out - Club Zanzibar. What wonderful memories come to mind at just the mention of its name. It was considered one of the most popular night spots in New York during that time; most of us had never been to a place with such a rousing bustle of entertainment. We drank and danced our weekend away, charming young women with our being called to duty. At that time soldiers were celebrated and called heroes and we loved the attention! Being with my men at this time and remembering the good camaraderie we shared has kept these moments alive for me. Toward the end of our leave, we all gathered back at the Commodore and over drinks we vowed to relive this time again once our tour of duty was over. Although we didn't express it, we knew there was a good chance that not all of us would make it back for that second leave to New York.

Those two nights in New York were quite a load for us. Exhausted and penniless, we were ready to go back to Camp Kilmer to rest and to get on with our fate. With the fun of the weekend behind us, we now became impatient. We invested too much in our training to not be able to test our grit. Where's that damned boat?

THE USAT *ALEXANDER*

On November 24th in 1944, troops boarded a train for the Port of New York City. From there, ferries took us and our personal gear to a dock where the massive ship awaited us. The USAT *Alexander* was a story in itself. It was built in 1905, preceding the Titanic, and had an interesting history. First it was known as the *"Amerika"*, a passenger ship, when it belonged to its original German owners. After being seized by the Americans in 1917, it was converted into a troop ship for WWI and now WWII. On this journey it would contain some 5,000 men with their equipment.

The whole operation of transferring soldiers and equipment from the trains to the ship was well-planned and conducted by the Merchant Marines, the auxiliary arm of the US Navy. What could have been mass confusion turned into an orderly and timely transfer from the dock. On board, each unit was assigned to its own company area where they quickly located their bunks and collapsed to continue their "withdrawal" from the New York City festivities. From that point on, any resemblance to an ocean cruise was non-existent.

What should have been the continuation of an amazing adventure for me, instead became a nightmare. From the moment the ship cleared New York Harbor, and the waves of the Atlantic began to beat against the hull of the ship, I was seasick. Now, for those of you who have never experienced seasickness continuously for two weeks, there is no understanding of the depth to which one can sink during its course. Death would have been welcome! Food, for the most part, was out of the question – it just wouldn't stay down. Trying to carry on duties helped some, but for the most part, my fifteen days on board ship were spent either on my backside or in the "head" – our slang for the bathroom.

Those who had sea legs had a fairly comfortable life aboard ship with plenty of sack time, poker games, or other opportunities. On board there was a library, a PX, and lots of movies playing at a makeshift theatre; and, as I heard, there were long lines at each. The weather was good so most of the men enjoyed going up to the deck for fresh air. On one of my few attempts to venture topside, I was able to catch a glimpse of the unbelievable beauty of the Mediterranean Sea at night. What a treat for this country boy.

Meals were served twice daily at assigned times for each unit. Those who weren't infirmed looked forward to the meals. I heard the meals were quite good, given the circumstances, and were served on a platter and carried to a table at which the men would stand to eat. Not bad – until the person across the table from you let go of his "cookies" in your direction. Whatever sense of composure one might have gained at that point was quickly lost. Before you knew it, except for a few stalwart seamen, the whole room was vomiting, and it was back to the head, the bunk, or if you were lucky, topside.

The route for the ship, as with the troop trains, was designed to mislead the enemy. The ship soon joined others to make up a convoy with Navy ships leading and trailing for protection. Some days later, in the evening, we saw the Rock of Gibraltar and the next day, the coast of Africa. The new sightings changed everything. We were going to Europe! There was some relief among the men at this point. The Germans and Italians were considered more predictable and more civilized when compared to the Japanese. Too, the jungles and climate of the South Pacific weren't as attractive as the weather and environment on the European continent. If you could say we were happy about our destination, well, yes, we were happy.

Telling rumors and rumors-of-rumors were the principal occupation of the men during their long hours on the ship. It was amazing how some of the men played games with the minds of others. It turned into a kids game when a few of the soldiers started a game by circulating a trumped-up rumor just to see how long it would take for it to return to them and in what form it would be. Some rumors held that a bubonic plague germ was being dropped on the battlefield; others stated that soldiers would be charged for the artillery they would use. As officers we attempted to stem all the rumors by supplying information as quickly and as completely as it could be released. In truth, there were times we were kept in the dark as well. On the whole, our efforts were a complete failure. With too much time on their hands, the men believed what they wanted to believe and chose what they wanted to worry about.

On a daily basis, we held classes orienting servicemen on physical hygiene, articles of war, conduct in combat zones, etc., and held additional drills centering on abandoning the ship, fire drills, and other safety measures. These drills, while not all that reassuring, were taken in stride. Huge areas on the ship were designated for physical exercise routines, but training topside was what the men loved best. It was the only time they could legally go on deck to get fresh air and watch as the naval escort followed alongside us. Being part of a convoy gave us a more secure feeling since we had two or three submarine alerts during the voyage. Each alert was purported to be due to an air raid in the Mediterranean Sea. Other than those tense moments, the crossing was uneventful and the only complaints came from the seasickness and that it took thirteen days for a five or six day trip.

At long last the USAT *Alexander* arrived at the Port of Marseilles, France, but for some unknown reason, we weren't able to dock immediately. Instead we were resigned to stay within view of the port, hearing the occasional lone German plane being greeted by anti-aircraft fire above the bombed city. On December 9th, 1944 we were able to dock the ship. Even then, the penetrating cold air carried the sounds of war. It was our first glimpse of what was to be our destiny.

PART II: AT WAR

CHAPTER FOUR

AT WAR
MARSEILLES, FRANCE
DECEMBER 9, 1944

Thankfully, the USAT *Alexander* landed safely on the docks at Marseilles, France. Finally, we were off that damn boat and able to get our land-legs again! As happy as we were to get off the ship, we were looking at a grim sight. The misty, gray harbor at Marseilles was mutilated with what seemed like over two hundred sunken ships lying half out of the black water. The view was dismal as thousands of men solemnly marched off the ship carrying their back-packs and rifles and loaded onto trucks while little children scrambled after the soldiers, yelling:

"Have you any gum, chum?"

Troops were then convoyed twenty miles outside of the city, near Calas, France, to a staging area called Command Post 2 or CP2. Our stay here was solely for the purpose of distributing equipment to the troops and to finalize the organization of the units.

Upon arrival, GIs went directly to their assigned areas in a large barren field where they made their shelters and began a long, cold wait. Since each soldier was assigned shelter halves, which were the size of half of a tent, a few of the men became creative to make a bigger space. Two of the GIs would pitch their shelters together to make one small tent, giving them a little more room and they said it was a little more comfortable. When we bivouacked back in the States there had been plenty of pine boughs, leaves, straw, etc. to pad the floor of our tents. Not here! The entire barren ground was covered with rocks and frozen mud, making for an even more uncomfortable night's sleep. Worse yet, fires weren't allowed because the smoke would call attention to our location, so the men had to resign themselves to being cold and miserable with the brutal mists of freezing rain and snow.

GIs jumped at the opportunity to be on routine guard duty because it offered a chance to get out of the weather and duck into one of the big mess tents for a hot cup of coffee. In the upcoming months, these conditions, which we had initially thought were unbearable, proved to be a fairly normal way of living our lives in the service. We never got used to it, but we came to tolerate it.

I wasn't involved in the initial set-up of the command post but joined the troops later. Instead, I was given the directive to oversee the unloading of the equipment for the troops that was still on the ship. It was an important assignment and the opportunity to command the detail was a boost for my morale. I was put in charge of a company of Transportation Corps (supposedly specialists in the field) as they unloaded the ship and I was given eighteen hours to get the job done. I was feeling pretty good about myself and eager to prove my leadership. However, as my duty proceeded, I found that the terms "transportation corps" and "specialists" was just a fancy name given to the ship's crew that operated the cranes. Needless to say, they didn't take kindly to a nineteen year old, green, west Texas boy telling them what to do.

I began my assignment by organizing them to work alternately between the shelter of the ship's hold and on the dock so that the warmth of the hold could be shared among the men. It was a bitter, windy, and frigid 20° day. As time dragged on, I became concerned that the eighteen hours to unload the equipment would run much, much longer. At first, the job started off fairly steady. The hold crew loaded the equipment onto pallets. The pallets were then hoisted out of the hold onto the deck of the ship. They were then swung over onto the loading dock and unloaded onto two and a half ton trucks which departed for the command post. It seemed as if hundreds of trucks were lined up waiting to take the cargo. This went on slowly for hours. Suddenly, without any warning, the crew quit. Not a strike. They just sat down and quit with grumblings of "cold" and "too much work". They built fires on the deck (which was against all regulations) and despite my most vocal commands, refused to extinguish them. Over and over I talked with their non-commissioned officers trying to come up with some compromise that would remedy the situation. With heads shaking, fingers pointing, and lots of cajoling, talks went on for an hour or so with no results. I was at my wit's end and there was no question that a revolt was about to erupt when, magically, up came First Sergeant Dominey - the biggest and most dominant NCO I had ever seen! He seized command of the situation immediately by grabbing one of the main protesters by his throat and knocking him soundly to the dock floor and yelling, "Get your ass back to work!" The trouble-maker attempted to get up and fight back but after one look up into the eyes of the formidable Dominey, he decided it was better just to stay on the dock floor and listen. Then Dominey began cursing at the others, walking among them, shaking his fist in their faces while calling out all sorts of insults, oaths, and expressions. Miraculously, the crew got up, slowly put out the fires, and resumed their job. What a relief! I immediately allied with this super-human Dominey, coordinating details with him between the dock and the hold, but mostly seeing what I could do to help him. I made hourly inspections to see if everyone and every detail was in order and the work was progressing – and to always take hot coffee to Dominey!

During the unloading, a lone German bomber dropped bombs in Marseilles not far from the dock. The sound of the earsplitting explosions going off and the following air raids was pretty sobering to all of us and placed the unloading operation in its proper prospective. Immediately afterwards, my crew began to double-time their work and the task went much faster; however, my eighteen hour assignment took thirty hours. After completing the unloading of the hold area, I rejoined my troops at the command post, proud that another assignment was successfully completed (by the skin of my teeth - and the grace of one hell of a first sergeant).

ANTICS IN CP2

While at CP2, the officers were, once again, given favorable treatment by being quartered in a large tent that had a stove in it. We all had bunks with sleeping bags in which we rested as best we could. Even though these were still sparse accommodations, they were considerably more luxurious when compared to those under which the GIs were sleeping.

During this time, we all came to know Lieutenant Rene S. Davis, Company Executive Officer or "Dave", as he was affectionately known. He suffered terribly from vertigo, a fact all the fellows of his unit knew. Just how Dave was accepted into the Army was a mystery to all of us, although the fact that he had a relative that was a Surgeon General at one time may have had some bearing on it. We were pretty hard up for entertainment at the time, so a few of the guys decided to come up with their own way of amusing themselves. They asked the bugler to quietly awaken us all before he awakened Davis. After we were all up and surrounding Davis' bunk, the bugler sounded off with a blast. Davis' first move was to quickly rise in his sleeping bag, rest his weight on one elbow, whereupon he immediately would fall flat on his face! Eventually he would gather his wits and manage to sit up in his sleeping bag only to fall sideways, unmercifully hard on the ground with a resounding WHAP! Finally, he would make his way to his feet, put on his trousers, only to fall, stiff as a board to the ground with a bone crunching KWAP! All the while the entire tent of officers were rolling on the ground in convulsive laughter. As cruel as it sounds, these antics started our miserable day and Dave, being the good sport he was, didn't seem to mind at all and enjoyed the laugh with the rest of us!

Although Dave was a good sport, there was another soldier at CP2 that had a harder time – Corporal Albert Ackermann. Stateside, Ackermann had been an excellent soldier and was promoted to corporal over other well-qualified and deserving men. He had been recommended to OCS but for some reason had not been selected. While at Camp Kilmer, he had a complete change of heart for his part in the war. He sent out feelers to get himself out of his assigned division, but with no result. At CP2, he again continued his attempt to change his duties. One morning, Ackermann was ordered out of his tent to blow reveille, the customary bugle call to wake up military personnel. One step outside in the cold and Ackerman went back inside his tent, and while lying flat on his back in his sleeping bag, blew reveille from inside his tent! The commanding officer, seeing his laziness, jumped into the middle of his tent and made a mess of it. Finally, Ackermann got his wish. Someone from a higher-up position pulled him out of infantry and put him in Division Mail Service, a much easier and safer duty. He left us during the night and consequently left our squad one man short. The remaining men in his squad viewed him as a coward and loathed him for it. Fortunately, this type of cowardice wasn't a common occurrence so when it did happen, all the men took notice.

I was at CP2 a few days when I received orders to go into Marseilles with the Military Police to help with any problems the 42nd troops might be causing in town. My orders involved going into some parts of the city which were off limits and apprehend young GIs who were on a lark, ignoring their commands, and causing themselves a lot of trouble. Unfortunately, we had to pick up far too many of these wayward men and they were punished for their exploits.

During the day as we drove around Marseilles, I got my first taste of the true colors of the Red Cross. One afternoon I came upon one of their trucks where they charged our men five cents each for a donut, coffee, or cigarette (a fair amount of money at the time, especially on a soldier's salary). I was furious they would profit from the soldiers that were risking their lives to defend our country. To this day, I still harbor that resentment. History would later disclose that in charging the GIs, the Red Cross were only following orders given by the US Secretary of War.

While officers and non-coms remained busy making arrangements and planning our strategies, a second bomb scare came when a lone dive bomber shelled the city, causing huge fires. Other than this incident, it was a boring and miserable experience for the men waiting around in freezing conditions while we awaited our next move.

CHAPTER FIVE

ON TO THE FRONT
DECEMBER 15, 1944

On December 15th, we received the call to "move out". There had been a retreat in the fighting in the Belgium sector according to the limited news reports we received. Acting as part of Task Force Linden, we assumed we were headed to support and relieve the units in the Battle of the Bulge.

Units of GIs left command post on December 21st and were loaded onto boxcars heading for the front line. The boxcars were nicknamed "forty-and-eight" railcars for the WWI boxcars which could hold either forty men or eight horses. All that was certain to us at this point was that the horrible conditions of the boxcars hadn't changed from the time they were used in World War I. They were cold, windy, and unmercifully uncomfortable as we struggled for footing. The only relief came when the train halted long enough for the troops to unload, stretch, and walk. Unannounced, the train would slowly start up again, leaving a mad scramble of all the men rushing to get back on the train before it left them behind. The train headed north as hours ran into days and the nights were colder than we had ever experienced before. After three days of riding in the railcars, we arrived at Domnom-lès-Dieuze, France and changed from the forty-and-eight railcars to the back of trucks for transportation as we traveled in convoys. Again, our direction changed to the northeast and we still had no indication of our destination. Our new transportation proved to be somewhat better than the miserable railcars. The trucks were covered so they mercifully kept some of the snow, rain, and wind off of us during the bumpy ride. Still, we always looked forward to the time we could dismount from the trucks for occasional stretches and eat a meal.

We had been eating K-rations since being at the command post outside of Marseilles, but now we were given the more desirable C-rations. The C-rations consisted of cans containing larger portions and could be divided among three or four men. They always seemed more palatable with added variety. On our stops along the way, GIs would take the opportunity to contact local civilians and trade their K-rations and cigarettes for wine and other things. This was strictly against regulations, but it was overlooked to some extent because of the situation. The drive had a few notable moments when an officer would have to stop the convoy to remove a mademoiselle or two who had been talked into traveling with us and stowed away in the trucks. For the most part, we were only eighteen or nineteen year old kids and at times we acted as such. I've got to say that despite the interruption it broke the monotony of the trip!

On our ride to the front, we saw the devastation that combat had left behind. We saw wrecked tanks, field rifles, trucks, and equipment left on the side of the road that had once been new but were now junk with a trace of rust beginning to show. Trucks loaded with ragged, dirty, and dog-tired troops came from ahead and disappeared behind the convoy. Huge track equipment hauled beat-up tanks and armored vehicles for repairs so they could re-enter the combat that lay ahead. As our convoy made temporary stops en route, there were exchanges of light banter between the seasoned soldiers coming from the front and the rookies that were now heading there to take their place. The news was both good and bad, both comforting and disconcerting. The air was somewhat lightened by the veterans reminding the inexperienced troops, "Don't forget to duck!"

The plan for the regiments of Task Force Linden was to move into the Bulge to support the troops who were trapped in a massive attack by German forces, numbering far more than the Allies. The terrain slowly turned into a thick forest with snow falling continuously and the ground and trees were covered with snow. We drove on narrow forest roads that were crowded with troops coming and going, with more signs of battle having taken place all along the route.

At some point, we heard that the situation at the Bulge had changed due to a break in the weather, and Task Force Linden was to turn back from our stated mission and move to a new location to help the 7th Army in Alsace. Changing locations and assignments happened a lot during the war; as the action changed, so did we. We seldom knew exactly where we were going and for how long. We proceeded to reverse our course by going back through Domnom-lès-Dieuze, France, and take a new direction – south. The terrain changed from snowy, wooded mountains to flat open country. As the snow stopped and the visibility opened, the weather seemed warmer. It raised our spirits and we hoped it was a good omen.

On the evening of December 24th, our convoy crawled around the outskirts of Strasbourg, France. We had only read about the quaint little Alsace village and were totally unprepared for its larger size. We found our way through the darkened streets with no sign of life or movement. The quiet of the village was eerie and it impressed us as being very odd – unusual at best, for we had become familiar with the active French villages we had passed before. Now, no one was moving about and the lights were out; the only noise you heard was our trucks and their tires crushing the snow on the icy road. On one of our breaks, we heard rumors of an infantrymen from another division who had been killed when, during a brief stop, he saw a German helmet on the side of the road and had run to grab it as a souvenir. The helmet had been booby trapped and exploded when he picked it up. It was another reminder to all of us to never, ever, let our guard down. The convoy continued, skirting most of the city, winding through changing terrain, and finally came to a halt at Fort Kronprinz at 3 pm on the 24th of December in 1944.

Fort Kronprinz was one of several forts built around Strasbourg, and was situated along the Maginot Line on the Rhine River. The Maginot Line is a line of fortresses, pill boxes, and bunkers which the French had formed right after the Franco Prussian War. The fort was surrounded by a deep, wide concrete trench, possibly twenty feet wide, with a barbed wire entanglement surrounding it. The inside of the fort was dark and dank from the humidity. It hadn't been maintained at all and was filthy. As soon as we arrived, we went to assigned foxholes and assumed guard duties that included patrolling the upper banks of the Rhine. A German army was just across the river, ready to cross at any time. During the nights there was intermittent shelling by both sides, but gratefully, we could hear the comforting drone of our support bombers flying overhead giving us a degree of safety while we defended our position.

My memory clearly pictures the dark nights of icy fog hanging in the air over the Rhine. Any movement at all was dangerous and all of the troops were nervous. We were given a different password each night so the men who were in patrols and on guard were able to identify their own comrades through the darkness and fog. You could slightly hear the whisper of the password as a soldier moved through the area. Though our positions in foxholes were secure, anyone outside of it was fair game whether you had a password or not. By now, the Germans knew our passwords better than we did. From our vantage point, we could see their patrols moving up and down the river, their silhouettes moving stealthily across the Rhine. We could even hear the movement of tanks as they repositioned themselves. It was gloomy with no moon or stars to give us light. The weather was below freezing, drizzling sleet, and snow showers were coming from the endless overcast sky. Shelling was sporadic, most of it landing behind the lines. I remember Sergeant Geary advising me, "Always fall on your back, so you can see what is going on above you." I don't know if I ever really used his advice, but it was good to know just the same.

FIGHTING POWER

During our months of training in the States, we had plenty of time to learn how to use our equipment. But now that we were on the front line, we needed to learn the equipment of our adversaries. The Germans had a variety of threatening equipment, but of them all, the Tiger tank was the most memorable. More than any other tank in World War II, it was known for its impenetrable armor and its highly accurate 88mm gun. Only a lucky shot at the tract suspension system could knock it out. Characteristic as well as chilling and unforgettable, was the sound of its diesel engines and the squeaking and clanking of its track system while it was moving. We dreaded hearing them maneuver at night. The Tiger's sound echoing in the night would tense even the most seasoned GI, for it was the Germans' most effective instrument of war.

America's M-4 Sherman tanks and their 76mm lower muzzle velocity cannon was our counterpart to the Tiger, but it was inferior to it and unfortunately this was proven time and time again. The only reason we were more successful than the Germans was because we outnumbered them with our tank corps.

The Germans' "burp gun" was another one of their superior weapons. It had a fantastically fast rate of fire and although it wasn't accurate, it was dependable and the sound of one firing was intimidating, to say the least. As time progressed, more and more of the GIs chose to use them over our own equipment. Whenever a German soldier was killed, we would simply drop our own rifle and pick up their firearm to use. Some of the American GIs carried BARs (Browning Automatic Rifle); and when they could handle the extra weight, they would carry a bazooka or two. The ammunition for the bazookas was cumbersome and heavy, especially when we were also towing the 57mm A/T guns.

It didn't take long for me to recognize that I needed more fire power if I was going to be an effective soldier. I put my M1911 .45 caliber pistol and M1 .30 caliber carbine away and carried an

M1 Garand rifle. I found the M1911 completely ineffective and limited in its accuracy while the M1 provided a good amount of fire power. It was as practical a weapon that I had been trained in, and I had attained the degree of "Expert Marksman" with it. I could strip the M1 in the dark with no trouble. And, to tell the truth, I wanted to be as inconspicuous as was practical.

Some of the men carried "Tommy" guns. I was hesitant to carry one because they were so dangerous. They were quick on the trigger and risky. We also had "grease guns", a .45 caliber weapon, during the latter part of the war. It was a practical weapon, but I didn't carry one of those either; they were prone to jam at the last minute, and I wouldn't risk it. As a rule I also carried two or more phosphorous hand grenades. Easily available to us in large quantities, the phosphorus grenade would burst with a wide band of white smoke that would either signal our location or, if necessary, would screen our movements if we were in close contact with a German.

THOUGHTS OF CHRISTMAS

The Maginot Line was continually being penetrated by the Germans. Their patrols were highly disciplined in their furtive movements and they could erupt in a firefight in a moment, then disappear the next. There was just enough snow on the ground for them to blend in with their camouflaged white suits. But, they had a flaw – the smell of their artificial tobacco they smoked, ersatz, clung to their uniforms. It had a terrible odor and we could smell it long before we saw them.

As their mortars kept us pinned down and hunkered in our foxholes, I became lost in my thoughts and it dawned on me that it was nearing Christmas and I wouldn't be with my family during the warmth and cheer of the holidays. I always knew the reality of it, but the full impact came upon me. I had always been at home on Christmas and I immediately became homesick. I had no choice but to quickly shrug off my despair because now, at twenty years of age, I had thirty three men looking for me to lead them. Like me, they too were far from home on the holidays and desperately homesick.

RELIGION IN THE FOXHOLE

The expression, "There are no atheists in foxholes", holds more truth than poetry. There are always those GIs who are religious from their upbringing and never wavered. And then, there are those who once they left home would relax their attentions and morals. But, I've found that when confronted with the imminent dangers of war, a soldier's relationship with his God becomes powerful and more significant. In the 222nd Regiment, there was a Protestant chaplain, a Catholic priest, and a rabbi to serve every spiritual need of the GI. With my Presbyterian upbringing, I became familiar with Captain James A. Connett, the chaplain. He was an unusual man being somewhat older than the norm for officers; he was probably in his late twenties. An impressive looking man, he was highly intelligent with a nice personality, had an almost stately presence, and a real dedication to his calling. Even though he was a Yankee and I was a southern boy, Connett soon became a friend and a confidant. He conducted services which always seemed to be expressly for the moment.

The rabbi, Captain Eli A. Bohnen differed from Connett in that he was a gentle person, quiet spoken, and was able to provide empathy in any given situation. He too, became a friend to all the officers and men, whether they were Catholic, Protestant, or Jewish. These religious figures did a remarkable job during a difficult time and always turned up in the most unusual places at the most extraordinary times to minister to their flocks. In addition to comforting the wounded, giving last rites, and providing comfort to the front line GIs, they held regular services in any type of situation and under any sort of circumstance. You could find them holding services in a quaint French Cathedral at one of the dorfs on our stops, or hunkered down in a foxhole as bullets ricocheted above our heads. There were many times when you found them helping the medics as stretcher bearers. A particular memory I'll never forget is the picture of Bohnen, first giving comfort to an injured soldier and then, tragically, the soldier's last rites. The grief he showed in his tears and the sincerity in his pleading with the Almighty appeared in the beautiful expression of compassion on his face. Enough cannot be credited to these men of God and the good they accomplished. There was reassurance in realizing that man cannot get all that far from his deep-seated beliefs, no matter how he might try to conceal this softer side.

It's interesting to note here that our medic, "Doc" Horton, was a conscientious objector – a Seventh Day Adventist, who wasn't afraid of the Devil himself. We respected him as he worked tirelessly beside us for our entire time during battle.

CHRISTMAS ON THE FRONT

Surprisingly, Christmas Day 1944 was almost festive. While there was little slackening of shelling, other activities were reduced on both sides. The security inside Fort Kronprinz allowed us to have a hot turkey dinner with all the trimmings. Even the outposts were relieved so they too could enjoy the wondrous reprieve from their daily rations. We all joked that it was "the Last Supper."

I celebrated Christmas with those who I now considered my friends. At midnight we gathered in a gloomy, small chapel located in an underground room far to the rear of the fort for a service conducted by Chaplain Connett. It was one of the more profound services I have ever heard. As we sat on benches quietly listening to Connett's words, carrying our M1s on our laps and with the constant noise of the shelling as our background, the reality of our situation sunk into all of us and never left our minds during the service.

That momentary sense of calm was not to last. Late that night of the 25th, our semi-quiet spell was broken when the Germans made a forceful thrust across the river. All hell broke loose with nightmarish confusion among the newer "green" troops. There were German patrols all over the place but it was the 3rd Battalion which took on the fight. German loudspeakers from across the river mockingly welcomed the 42nd and warned us of what was to take place next.

The next day, a member of my platoon, having experienced the proximity of the sights and sounds of war, went berserk at one of the gun positions while guarding the line. Two soldiers manning the anti-tank guns alongside him left their positions to find me and advise me of the situation. I immediately wound my way up the hill to the gun position to check on him. We found that he had gone temporarily insane, yelling, talking to himself and aiming his gun at imaginary Germans. He threatened to shoot both me and his fellow soldiers at the least provocation. Because of his loud antics, he was fortunate he hadn't been targeted and killed by German fire. We coaxed him back to the command post at Fort Kronprinz as best we could as he struggled through the deep snow and ice.

Back at the fort, we warmed him up and put him to bed. By the next morning, other than being confused as to what had happened, he had snapped out of it. I never knew whether it was the extreme cold (it was $20°$ Fahrenheit at the time) or the frightening battles we were in such proximity to that caused his condition, but from that point on I began to realize how combat could affect a man mentally. This particular soldier would go on to earn a Bronze Star for valor, undoubtedly saving lives with his courage and quick thinking.

Over the next few days we lived through more thrusts by the full brunt of German supporting tank units, and two battalions of SS troops who came across the river to deliver a crippling blow to the Task Force and the 79th Infantry Division who were known as "The Cross of Lorraine". At the time, my platoon, the 2nd Platoon of A/T, was now acting in the role of riflemen and were attached to Company A. After what seemed like days of back and forth warfare, the Germans were fortunately contained and withdrew back across the Rhine to the small dorf of Kehl.

CHICKEN COOPS AND GOUMIERS

On December 28, 1944 our headquarters was moved from the Maginot Line at Fort Kronprinz to Wolfisheim, France, a suburb of

Strasbourg. While we were in reserve, the A/T'ers tackled different responsibilities. We were put in charge of patrolling the streets of Strasbourg where we suspected some civilians were working with the enemy. The dark and deserted city felt as if it had eyes everywhere you went. Even though a stiff curfew was enforced, there was always the threat of a German patrol or sniper having made their way into the city to attack an American patrol without any warning. We knew this had happened several times to the 7th Army troops in the city, and wanted to make sure this didn't happen to us.

As New Year's Eve blew in, the 2nd Platoon moved on to Illkirch-Graffenstaden, France to support the Free French First Army unit. The unit had previously been hurt by German feeler attacks and it needed extra support. As luck would have it, our 2nd Platoon was chosen to be that support. As we arrived into their encampment, it seemed that the First Free French lacked some organization. Their troops were slovenly, dirty, and disorganized to the point you would think they were on a picnic. Their tanks, furnished by the US, rolled in with chicken coops on the turret, clothes hanging from the radio antennae, and with women accompanying the troops. They appeared to lack discipline but as history would show they were the most decorated division of the French Army - so they did not lack the fighting spirit.

A small group of Moroccan soldiers, called Goumiers, fought as part of the French forces and convoyed with them on their assignments. The Goumiers were giant men, with many standing over six feet tall and weighing as much as three hundred pounds. They were typically dressed in distinctive uniforms of turbans and sashes with baggy trousers and they carried cruel-looking curved knives, called jambiyas. It didn't take long for stories to circulate among the troops to not move too widely at night. In one incident, a GI was grabbed from behind by one of the Moroccans who held a knife at his throat until the Moroccan identified him by smell. The Goumier then disappeared as silently as he had appeared.

There was nothing that could be done with the Free French Forces except to cover for them as best we could. Fortunately there was little patrolling by the enemy during that time. It was good news when we heard that we were moving from their sector and on to the Rhineland in southwestern Germany to give support to the 7th Army.

We wanted nothing to do with them.

OPERATION NORDWIND

Beginning on December 31, 1944 a German offensive code named "Operation Nordwind", directed by Hitler to "... exterminate the enemy forces wherever we find them", and led by German Army commander General Johannes Blaskowitz, one of Germany's most infamous and threatening commanders, was launched against the 7th Army front on the border of southwestern Germany and northeastern France. Our front was at risk due to the heavy Allied losses, the limited number of American troops, and the presence of inexperienced troops that had just arrived. Taking advantage of our vulnerability along the 7th Army front, their timing was perfect.

We were spread thin on the front line with Germans to our front, and pockets of German units penetrating right through our lines. Immediately to the task force front was the 19th German Army. Tasked to envelop us from behind was the 1st German Army's 90th Corps, who had the goal of linking up with the 19th German Army at Saverne – thereby destroying our Army group and recapturing an area important to Hitler's efforts. The jewel of his plan was to regain Strasbourg, a politically significant objective.

Eisenhower ordered elements of the 79th Infantry and 14th Armored Division to withdraw from Rittershoffen and to occupy new positions on the south bank of the Moder River, giving up territory that was valuable, hard-gained and would have to be retaken.

AMERICANS NEVER RETREAT?

"Americans never retreat!" That's the motto ... except we do. A more heroic term is, "strategic withdrawal to adjust positions for the tactical situation of the moment." During the time of Operation Nordwind, it was clear that the enemy's strengthening was for the purpose of making a thrust into our front lines. The 7th Army lines were so severely extended that new positions had to be taken to the rear where lines could be shortened and more defensible. My platoon was ordered to hold its position on the front lines until 1300 hours and then withdraw to the rear to a new Main Line of Resistance (MLR). A runner changed these orders at 1100 to make the pullout begin at 1200. It was snowing heavily when the time came. Getting the guns out of their emplacements was next to impossible with solid ice forming around them. It was a laborious effort and without a doubt, the enemy had a full picture of what was taking place.

Moving to the rear was slow because our passageway was blocked by hundreds, perhaps thousands, of civilians escaping the area. They trudged on the icy roads with their horse-drawn carts, buggies, bicycles, and any other sort of transportation they could find. Most of the poor souls walked in ragged clothes with shoes unfit for the deep snow and ice, carrying heavy loads of weathered bags of their belongings. Babies were crying from the cold and hunger as their mothers held them deep to their chest to keep them warm. The heartbreak of the sight took a toll on all of us. Their suffering in the bitter cold was worse than ours because they were so ill-clothed, hungry, and suffering from their own loss.

All day and all night we trudged through the snow at a snail's pace trying to get through the lines of troops to the rear. A number of times, small units of troops would pass through our unit also on their way to the rear, having fulfilled their mission and being reassigned to another position. The 2nd Platoon never found the new MLR as it wasn't recognizable in all the confusion and weather. German patrols were following us but chose not to engage us for some merciful reason.

We assumed they were just trying to identify the new positions that would be our new MLR.

My troops' situation soon changed so that the 222nd could cover a division front. The 2nd Platoon, then attached to Company C, had its front along a ridge made by the Maginot Line immediately west of Hunspach, France (in the Alsace region). For reasons I didn't understand, guns were placed on the eastern (or forward) slope at points with little or no possibility of safely pulling out in the event of a tank attack. The men were spaced in foxholes along the front where communications were poor and even our sound-powered phones provided little communication between the gun positions and headquarters. It was a dangerous and unpredictable place to be and the troops were scared to death.

Our unit was shelled by artillery, sending us a clear message that we were getting close to a fight. By now, the glamour of being at war had long faded, our comradeship had worn thin, and our cold and discomfort were intolerable. I remember very clearly the conversation I had with my father before I signed on for battle when he urged me to try for a state-side job and stay away from combat. I was sincere when I assured him that I had to go and do my part. But, as I lay flat on my stomach on the frozen ground alongside the road, with shells falling around me, deafening and powerfully shaking the earth, I remembered my commitment to my dad and muttered out loud, "Dad, you were right once more!" No one heard. I was cold, frustrated, and scared.

On one occasion General Linden came to the front on an inspection. It was during the bitterest of winter days when he came up to my foxhole. I remember I was flustered on looking up and seeing the stars on his uniform. As I recall, I stood up, saluted, and gave some sort of a report. I remember that he seemed very sympathetic of our situation. During the short time he was there, an assault of incoming artillery came rushing in, prompting him to jump into the same foxhole I was in. We were crowded together, but under the circumstances, I didn't care that he was General Linden and I was a lowly 2nd Lieutenant. Rank didn't make any difference while we hunkered down in the icy mud as shells flew over our heads. It seemed like hours but it was probably only minutes. As the incoming artillery slowed to a halt, General Linden climbed out of the hole and said, "Carry on."

At night as we lay in our foxholes, we could hear the movement of troops, trucks, and tanks; and, with no wind, we could easily hear the Germans talking to one another. During the day there were occasional lulls in mortar fire during which time an unlucky rabbit or two could be seen in the valley. Both sides would fire on the rabbit but as far as we could tell, none were ever hit. I wondered whether the target was for food or fun, but all the same, none of my men would have risked going into the valley to get the poor rabbit even if it had fallen from the ambush.

With forces on both sides of the valley, it was ironic how picturesque and beautiful the scene was with a backdrop of a church steeple and small buildings of the dorf, Ingolsheim. Unfortunately, the steeple didn't last long. We suspected the Germans were using it for an observation post and had a sniper sitting at the windows ready to take out any unsuspecting GI. Our Anti-Tank guns aimed, fired, and watched as the steeple collapsed –it was a sad but necessary cost of the war.

PATROLLING

There were generally two types of patrols - combat and reconnaissance. Combat patrols were conducted to kill or capture enemy soldiers, gather equipment, or to destroy installations and facilities. Reconnaissance patrols were conducted to gather information on the location and tactics of the enemy and to verify any information that we had previously received. It was an extremely dangerous patrol in that most times the scouts would be on their stomachs inching their way within earshot of the enemy in their trenches.

A few officers took the patrol assignments in stride or at least they said they did. I never did. I couldn't. Patrolling was a suicide mission;

three or more men ventured behind enemy lines while the enemy was in their camp fully expecting, even waiting, for our patrol activities. Nonetheless, patrols were an important part of the battle.

One of the first things to take place prior to a patrol assignment was to attend an orientation. An officer from S-2 (Battalion Intelligence Section) would gather the men that had been chosen for the duty, define the type of patrol, and outline their mission. The officer would then provide them a study of the route, tell them what to expect, and give them a time schedule. The men would then go over a myriad of intricate information to prepare themselves for any set of circumstances. In nearly every instance, the orientation, though necessary, never provided for the situations the GI would encounter. Each officer guiding the group was given a code name to use during the patrolling; mine was "Baker Catcher".

After the orientation, the patrol prepared for all the details focusing on how to minimize making any noise, and how to reduce any possibility of attracting the attention of the enemy. Once we began our trek into enemy lines, we would crawl at a snail's pace from one cover to another and then pause for the remainder of the men to move up. In the dark of night, we wouldn't talk or even whisper and only used arm and hand signals to communicate. The slow movement through the snow and mud was numbing and we were scared to death. Yet, being scared paid off; the fear of the situation would prompt us to use more caution and prevent carelessness. Lying in the snow, rain or mud, listening for hours trying to learn the location of the Germans, trying to understand what was taking place, keeping track of numbers, places, and times, took a toll on every soldier who made the journey.

No two patrols ever had the same experience. The changes of the terrain, disposition of the enemy, hidden land mines and booby traps, or even friendly artillery could change from one day to the next. Following the proposed plan of action was almost always impossible and many times the route didn't match what the S2 had laid out. Detours had to be made whenever we felt the Germans were suspicious we might be near, then we would take long pauses lying flat in the snow for several hours waiting for the time to come when we could feel safe enough to move on with our orders. Freezing, doubting, praying, wishing, damning - all of these things came into our minds as we patrolled. I was acutely aware that the men in my patrol were looking for guidance and confidence in my being able to handle the situation. Little did my men know their leader was just as scared.

Our missions on patrol were seldom fully accomplished. It was difficult enough for the men to move through the enemy's lines, much less to do so in planned routes with planned timing, and rendezvous at a predetermined location. Unexpected changes in plans and time schedules were pretty much the routine so there never was time to do everything. At some point, the soundless "nod" came from the officer or leader of the patrol, designating "time to return", and we would hurriedly retreat to friendly lines before we could be exposed by the dawn. Ironically, the men on patrols considered returning to their own lines as the most dangerous part of the operation. Returning GIs were trigger-happy and excitable and almost in a panic to get back. At the same time, nervous sentries guarding our lines often fired on any movement in front of them no matter how small, and as a result caused casualties to their own men. Security was so tight that passwords never seemed to be good enough to get past our sentries and there was always some other lengthy identification required. Every effort was made in the Army to simplify everything, but unfortunately, it invariably made things more complicated. Patrolling was one area when this should not have been the case, but it was.

Immediately after returning, the GIs from the patrol had to report to headquarters and go through a lengthy and wearisome debriefing. They were numb, cold, tired and barely able to stay awake for the investigation and yet they were interrogated by officers who were trained to get information out of each member of the patrol. The process would last for an hour, three hours, or until the patrol member would all but revolt or go to sleep on his feet. Having made only three such reconnaissance patrols, I found myself offering a prayer of thanksgiving for making it back alive while trying to answer their questions in a half-sleep.

On the evening of January 5th, a unit of the 315th Infantry Regiment of the 79th Division passed through our line going on a combat patrol only to come back the next day badly shot up and minus a lot of men. Soon after, Major Walter J. Fellenz, 1st Battalion Commander, called on the 2nd Platoon to make a recon patrol. During training back at Camp Gruber, a minimum of time was spent on rifle tactics and none on patrolling. Our lack of training was not a question when it came to Fellenz assigning patrols. The major seemed to consider the 2nd Platoon as an outside unit from his battalion and he was prone to assign us the more disagreeable maneuvers. Fortunately, many of these never materialized because Captain Lester H. Lummus, commander of Company A, stepped up and dismissed the wild assignments.

With this aside, there were still those missions we had to commit to patrol. On one occasion, I led a patrol on an overnight excursion that yielded little information of any value, but stirred up a considerable firefight that almost cost us our lives. We were only saved because the Germans became confused on our location and couldn't find us. They had assumed we were retreating on a particular route but in reality we skirted their squads and continued going deeper into enemy territory until we could make a safe turn-around and head back to our lines.

On another combat patrol led by Staff Sergeant Ivan M. Jones, my 1st Squad leader, a German flare was tripped, illuminating their position for the Germans. Fortunately, they were able to elude the Germans by laying in place in the deep snow for four hours, without movement, then returning to their lines when the heavy snowfall blocked visibility.

We were constantly having to convince our men that as risky as it was, patrolling provided critical intelligence information which later made our activities safer and more successful. It was considered the most dangerous of the GI's duties - not even second to heavy combat.

The Germans responded to our patrolling by heavy patrolling of their own. They were stealthy and well disciplined and could easily penetrate the coverage by our troops. We fired flares at night from time to time but the Germans knew how to keep their locations from being revealed. Occasionally, a German patrol would be located and we would engage in small arms fire. The next morning, tracks could be found but never the bodies. On several occasions when the snow let up, we could see ribbons of blood being stretched across the snow.

Around dawn on January 16th, a combat patrol from the 68th Armored Infantry Battalion moved through our lines after having been cut down in the foothills across the valley. The cold was a bitter and fierce enemy for them, and yet the protective cover of heavy snowfall kept their patrol unit from being completely wiped out. The poor guys wearing old combat boots and no overcoats were suffering from severe frostbite and had walked into everything our patrol had previously pointed out and reported. I remember the attitude of one sergeant who vowed to kill his commanding officer for committing them to a patrol when they had already read the reports and knew about the German strengths and equipment in the area.

CHAPTER SIX

THE LAST STRAW
HUNSPACH, FRANCE
JANUARY, 1945

Behind the 2nd Platoon's gun position in Hunspach, France, and on the back slope of the Maginot Line was a home with an old barn which had been used as quarters for an army workforce at some time in the past. The house and out-buildings were brick with tile roofs, substantially built and quite comfortable. It was the perfect size and ideal for quartering a platoon of men comfortably. My platoon took possession of the home – happy to find a warm place out of the weather. It had five rooms, four of which we commandeered, leaving the kitchen for the owner, his wife, and three children to live in. We quickly settled in, making ourselves at home with the help of the owner. He was a good-natured man, forty five years old, with a younger wife. They had three young children that were about six, four, and two years old. They were a sweet family and we appreciated the situation they found themselves in, and we were respectful of their needs.

The position of our outpost on the front line was such that we could only be relieved at night to avoid being seen by the Germans. Both the home and its surrounding barn and sheds were about a quarter of a mile downhill from our foxholes, making for an icy and strenuous walk plowing upward through the deep snow at night going to our positions, but it was always an easy walk downward as we looked forward to going back to share our misery with one another and to enjoy the home's comforts.

Having been in this position before, the old man and his family were immediately accommodating to us and kept plenty of wood in the fireplaces to keep us warm and furnished all the red wine and schnapps we wanted. Sometimes it seemed as if they knew what we needed even before we did. We always gave him plenty of tobacco from our rations and in return he looked after everyone as best he could.

His wife also took special care of us. There was an abundance of apples in their cellar and she would take flour and sugar, which the fellows magically found, and made the best apple strudel you could imagine. What a treat after being on prepared rations for so long! I think one of the reasons the family was friendly with us was because we shared our rations. We had a good arrangement with them and the men appreciated their hospitality and in turn, the family was able to eat better than they had in years.

We were amazed at how the old man and his family accepted the situation in which they found themselves. For example, during gunfire by German artillery, which was almost hourly, a short round hit his roof, knocking off many of the tiles. His response was simply to fix it with no grumbling or complaining. One day his prized possession, a milk cow, stepped on a mine and was killed. The old timer butchered the cow, never changing expression and accepted his fate as reality. Another day a mortar round hit and exploded, badly hurting his youngest daughter as she played out back of the house in the snow. We ran to get our medic and first aid supplies and the couple doctored the child as best they could. Once again, the couple accepted their fate. It was difficult to read just how they may have felt as they showed no emotion whatsoever.

Then came the day when a dud artillery shell came through the roof of the room that held his liquor still, making an irreparable hole in his copper still settling basin. This seemed to be the last straw for the old man. He sat down and openly wept without shame. It had all come to a head and he just couldn't cope with the situation further. He wasn't the same after that. Something had been taken out of him and he just gave up. "Das ist kreig".

This is war.

CHAPTER SEVEN

LIFE AT THE FRONT

All of the boot camps and the trainings we did in the United States could never have prepared us for the daily aspects of life we would live once we were in combat. But once we accepted our circumstances of the cold, the boxed food, and the complete lack of hygiene, the conditions were more tolerable. Or maybe I should say, the conditions were less sufferable. Regardless, this was a soldier's life, and we accepted it.

Food, for example, was a top priority for every GI. The adage that an army travels on its stomach is true. With the non-stop physical demands, plus the extreme cold, we needed lots of food to keep up our energy. Wisely, the Army had commandeered the Cracker Jack company to make up our K-rations with parcels of food, placing an entire meal in a Cracker Jack box. Now that seems like a tall order, but they did a good job considering the size of the miniscule boxes. There was a breakfast box which contained a can of bacon and eggs, a bar of dried fruit (prunes, apricots, raisins, apples, etc.), a packet of crackers, and a packet of instant coffee with packets of sugar and dried milk. For lunch, the box contained a small can of cheese and bacon, a packet of crackers, a packet of powdered lemonade, and a concentrated chocolate bar. At suppertime we opened the box to find a small can of potted ham, a packet of crackers, a packet of instant tea with lemon and sugar and another chocolate bar. All of the meals had enough calories to sustain us, but the small box seemed mighty meager for growing young men with big appetites.

The more desirable C-ration packs were designed to feed four or five men and were occasionally available. They consisted of canned peaches, canned meat (ham, roast beef, bacon, etc.), and other foods which were canned and preserved in quantities more in line with a soldier's appetite.

When we weren't eating the rations out of our boxes, the mess crew, under Corporal Phillip J. Polski did an excellent job feeding us. Besides taking care of our rations, the mess crew was also handy with their guns. More than once they dived into the battle when we came under attack. Thanks to Polski, the 2nd Platoon never went without food.

We did, however, have a surprise or two along the way that we appreciated. For instance, it was nothing short of remarkable how often hot meals were brought to the troops while we were dug into our foxholes. Complete meals were brought up and kept hot in insulated containers. In between these surprise meals, we existed on K- Rations for substance. Not knowing for sure where it all came from, we also relied on potato alcohol, which always seemed to be in plentiful supply. It didn't take long to learn that a short nip every hour or so would help to get the feeling back into our hands and feet. Canteens soon carried wine or schnapps on a regular basis. Five gallon water cans and even gasoline cans were also mustered into service. We took a lot of caution to not overdo the drinking for fear of not being able to function, but the warmth the alcohol gave us was priceless. I can say with confidence that not once was there a problem with one of the men over-drinking.

There were times when the lack of green vegetables was just too much for me. With my west Texas natural intuition, I would look for a broad leafed tree, take the leaves off and cook them in water in my steel helmet, adding a can of potted ham from my K-ration for seasoning. It wasn't exactly my mother's turnip greens but it seemed to satisfy my craving. After kidding me about my redneck efforts and then having a taste, many of the other fellows joined in trimming the trees of their leaves and boiling up their own concoction. (Cornbread was noticeably absent from the treat.)

Other aspects of our life on the front had some unwritten rules that we made sure to follow, one being that we never wore anything in the shape of insignias, colors, bars, or stripes on our uniform that would indicate our rank. We considered the decorated gold bar on our uniforms as an "aiming stake" for the Krauts, and discarded them as soon as we were in combat. Some of the officers wore their 1"x 3" stripe (identifying them as leaders) on the back of their helmets. At times they would muddy out the stripe on their helmet or swap for another helmet that didn't have the mark on it. We were fully aware that we might be captured at any time and we wanted to make it hard on the Germans to not distinguish our ranking. Some of the enlisted ranks would still wear their stripes and I always wondered if it wasn't their ego that caused them to make such a poor decision.

Our issues with food rations and emblems were both dealt with, but the opportunity to have a complete bowel movement (by not being interrupted) was at the top of our list of needs. Many of us drew the line at using the helmet for a bowel movement. Instead, we were careful to "squat and cover" – not always that easy to do considering some of the conditions we lived in and the nature of being in active combat. We did the best we could, but never found our opportunities very acceptable.

During World War I, the term "trench foot" was given to the foot damage most GIs became afflicted with from constantly standing in the cold, wet trenches. Clearly, the same condition was happening to many of the GIs while on the front lines during this war. It didn't take long for each of us to get into a program of continuously exchanging our wet socks for dry ones. When clean, dry socks weren't brought up with the chow, the men would put their wet socks inside their shirts to let their body heat dry them. Fortunately, most of the men in my unit were outfitted with boots containing waterproof shoepacks. These boots were a godsend with their wool-lined inserts that could easily be swapped out with another set. While trench foot could still be a problem with us, it didn't compare with the problems other units faced without the shoepacks.

CHAPTER EIGHT

SCHWEIGHAUSEN, FRANCE
JANUARY 21, 1945
7:00 AM

At 0700 on January 21st, the 2nd Platoon arrived at a position near Schweighausen-sur-Moder, France, to reunite with the remainder of the A/T Company. Almost immediately the 2nd Platoon was assigned to take up rifle positions in the MLR with A Company to prepare for another major thrust. The frigid weather was relentless, it felt almost inhuman. It was snowing and felt at least negative fifteen degrees. Mercifully, there wasn't any wind. Having no sleep for the past twenty four hours, we were dead on our feet. Most of the men chiseled foxholes from the frozen ground but a few of the fellows were so exhausted they chose to take the risk and sleep on the unprotected, frozen ground. As dangerous as this sounds, it was no problem to keep them alert and ready. Each soldier knew his situation and had made agreements with a buddy to take turns keeping guard during the night.

While in position at Schweighausen, tanks were put online to support us. No sooner had the tank been put into position when a storm of artillery and mortars came raining in on the tank. Some of the 2nd Platoon, including me, ran underneath the tank for cover, but when the artillery zeroed in on it, we ran for cover anywhere we could find. Almost immediately there was a direct hit on the tank killing the gunner and tank commander and wounding the driver. Those of us that had fled just missed a death sentence.

A major soon appeared on the scene wanting to retrieve the tank and asked if anyone could operate it. I had some experience in driving one while in basic training at Camp Hood and volunteered my help. I ran from my cover to the damaged tank. No sooner had I entered the hull (first repositioning those that were killed and wounded) and got into position, when the enemy's artillery and mortars began coming again. The direct hit had damaged the transmission of the tank so that it couldn't turn around or drive forward. With the incoming artillery exploding around me and after a few frantic moments trying to get the tank into gear, I was finally able to get into reverse and inch the broken-down tank off the slope and into a hidden area - but only did so after throwing up from the sheer fright of the moment. It was a long ten or fifteen minutes while I was in the Germans' zeroed in area - reminding me that I had once been told to "never volunteer for anything while in the Army".

That night, the German forces hit our lines trying to determine exactly where our MLR was located, but they were quickly repelled. A few hours later, some of the 222nd troops came through our lines after having been trapped the night before. Gratefully, they hadn't encountered the enemy troops which had just hit us and were in good shape. The MLR lines were continually adjusted forward and backward, from east to west and north to south, causing the weary soldiers to dig more foxholes and maneuver gun positions in the frozen ground. Few of the diggings were ever completed. The ground was so hard and iced over we could barely get our shovels in it; then, before we could make any use of it, we were repositioned. We were constantly moving so that the Germans would never get a hold on our location.

TRAGEDIES AND THE MILITARY SYSTEM

As history has shown us, war is a young person's game. Even though the younger soldier has more energy, strength and stamina, there are also disadvantages of an inexperienced mind. One detriment is the immaturity with which young GIs go into situations. Sometime during early 1945, a certain new recruit came to the company. He was given a too-short orientation and was then assigned to a squad and let loose. In only two hours after he arrived, he raped a German woman in her home nearby. The young soldier was arrested and locked up until his court martial. Sometime later he was found guilty and sentenced to twenty years in the United States Penitentiary at Fort Leavenworth, Kansas.

The misguided young soldier, with little training nor understanding of the Geneva Convention Agreement, came into the front lines thinking that as the victor, his spoils included everything he could take. Furthermore, being in the environment of the inhumanities of war, the soldier lost the meaning of being civilized. There were many, many, serious criminal acts committed by the American GIs which were never exposed, but the blatancy of this act had to be faced. A tragedy of this account was that the GI was completely at a loss as to why he was being arrested for having done something that, in his own mind, he considered perfectly acceptable and nothing more than "taking booty of war". His young life was consequently ruined because of the lack of moral guidance and discipline in his life – including right up to the time of committing the crime.

Injustice of the military system showed up again with a Pvt. Chapiro. At thirty nine years, he was considered an "old man" for the Army. He had eleven children at home and because of a childhood accident had only one eye. How could he have possibly been drafted? Prior to being shipped to France, every effort had been made through every channel available to have him discharged but with no results. By the time he arrived in Marseilles and then moved to the front line, he was a nervous wreck and cried every night, having an unnerving influence on the rest of us. We accepted him and each of us looked to take care of him the best we could. It wasn't until after the war in Europe was over that he was discharged. Chapiro was a good example of the unfairness of an older man being placed in the position of fulfilling a duty meant for a younger man – both physically and mentally.

SERGEANT KILROY

After the 222nd Infantry Regiment had been under constant attack for two or three days by the combined forces of Germany's 47th Volksgrenadier, the 7th Parachute and the 25th Panzer Divisions, the German infantry troops with both armor and heavy artillery moved forward to cut off our lead and retake a part of Alsace. After elements of the 7th Army withdrew, the Germans saw the opportunity to keep their momentum going. The 222nd, with a few thousand men, found themselves defending a front approximately 7,500 yards in length – an area normally defended by a division of men.

Communications were practically nil, the cold was bitter, and tree bursts from artillery shells canceled any security a GI could feel in his foxhole. Temperatures felt like minus twenty degrees during the night and the winds made it almost unbearable. Snow was two to three feet deep and our fox holes would fill with water about as fast as they could be bailed out, making sleep out of the question. We stayed completely silent, always seeking reassurance from the GI in the next foxhole. Hearing his whispers or prayers was always comforting. Our sense of smell became acute, as we waited for the odor of the Germans' ersatz tobacco. We were hesitant to use hand grenades because our own troops were moving in the dark and yet occasionally we would carefully use them. Fortunately, I can't remember any GIs being hit by our own grenades - a miracle in itself.

At dawn of January 25th, A Company moved out to regain territory given up the day before. Captain Lummus ordered us to remain in position. No sooner had the company moved out when Fellenz, 1st Battalion Commander, came up demanding to know why the 2nd had not gone with them. On learning of Lummus' orders, Major Fellenz ordered the 2nd Platoon to move out with A Company, leaving our 57mm guns abandoned and in position. The conflict of orders caused a lot of confusion among us, but Lummus was capable of rolling with the punches and asked us to do the same, so we headed out to join Company A. About this time, A Company encountered a unit of Germans advancing and once again there was mass chaos. Sgt. Jones, the leader of my 1st squad, and his nine men, knocked out an armored vehicle with bazookas. Lummus was so impressed with the new development, he nicknamed Jones "Sgt. Kilroy"! It became a name we always kidded him with.

Jones proved again his super powers the next day. I had just moved to one of his 57mm gun positions when German artillery started to hit the area. For some reason he insisted I move into a foxhole that had already been prepared. At his persistence, I jumped into the foxhole and he placed one of the side-pieces of an armor plate from our 57mm A/T gun over me. Almost immediately, an incoming mortar round landed directly on top of the armor plate. The explosion was transmitted by my helmet and went through my neck and down my spine, causing my neck to be forced downward between my shoulders. I was sure I would have spinal injuries, but shortly after the barrage had subsided, Jones helped me out of the foxhole (I was still so dazed I couldn't get my bearings) to view what had just taken place. The armor plate had a three inch dent caused by the explosion of the mortar shell! There was no question that Jones had saved my life that day. All I came away with was a sore neck, a dulled sense of hearing, and a terrific headache. I was able to see that Sgt Kilroy was awarded a Bronze Star for similar heroic actions later in March.

A Company, along with the 2nd Platoon in tow, forged forward and regained the dorf of Ohlungen, with orders to hold and defend it. As darkness came in, we heard the eerie clank-i-ty clank of a Tiger tank slowly moving along the edge of the community. Immediately, we moved our guns towards the location where we had heard the tank movement, expecting to take it out, but for some odd reason the Germans had pulled back.

We repositioned again and waited. During that night, the 14th Armored Division, after a relentless battle, trudged through Ohlungen going to their command post. I still remember the poor, worn out men coming through the snow without ample clothing, wearing combat boots instead of the warmer shoepacks. They passed through the lines as though they were zombies - not acknowledging our presence nor looking one way or another – just slowly staggering ahead.

At daybreak on the 26th, the Germans brought back the Tiger tank and another armored vehicle and hit us from behind. As a major battle broke out, we were unable to hit the tanks but fortunately we were able to hold our positions in Ohlungen and keep the dorf. Around 1400, the enemy pulled back and Lummus quickly sent troops out to occupy the ground. The wounded were gathered, some being treated on the spot while others were sent to field hospitals. There were a number of prisoners taken during that period and sent to Military Police located well in the rear.

After the attack, the 2nd Platoon was sent into an area northeast of Ohlungen, taking positions in the woods along a highway where we remained until the next day. The Germans were patrolling the area during the night and there was plenty of incoming artillery and tree bursts to keep us trigger-ready for the next fight. Our own patrols would pass through our lines during the night, making us jumpy and at times confused. Which were which? We simply didn't know who was coming nor did we have a password we could count on. All the while our SCR-536 radios were totally ineffective and the communications had to be carried out by runners or adjacent rifle platoons' walkie-talkies. It was another frightening situation.

By now the soldiers of the 222nd were pretty well used up, so when word came that we were going to be relieved by the 101st Airborne Division and sent to an Army reserve base, a place to rest and recoup, it was sweet news to our ears. The men's anticipation to leave the area went through the gamut of thoughts running from their worry about trench foot, how to get rid of lice - or what we called "cooties", to the longing for a good hot meal. Even with the good news it was hard to not be pessimistic. GIs worried they would be killed by tree bursts or rifle fire before they were relieved. Taking a break at an Army reserve base seemed too good to be true and something was bound to happen.

The men had a good point, for relief came slowly. The 101st Division was so depleted in manpower and equipment that there was some question as to whether they were even capable of replacing the 222nd. Though we waited until the evening to begin the switch, the enemy had discovered what was happening, and started shelling the MLR and the rear areas before we could get out. The darkness, lack of password, usual confusion of such a maneuver and carelessness of the fatigued soldiers added to our problems. But as time wore on we were mercifully able to pull out.

The 222 Infantry Regiment is cited for extraordinary and outstanding performance of duty in action against the enemy on 24 and 25 January 1945, in the Bois D'Ohlungen, and the vicinity of Schweighausen and Neuborg, France. The citation reads:

On the night of 24 January 1945, the 222nd Infantry Regiment, under strength by half a Battalion of riflemen, yet necessarily extended over a 7500-yard front, was attacked by five regiments from the 7th Parachute, 25th Panzer and 47th German VG Divisions which were supported by heavy artillery. Ordered to hold at all costs, the Regiment withstood the enemy's desperate bid to break the Seventh Army Moder River Line. Fighting back from ice-filled foxholes, the outnumbered defenders fought off wave after wave of enemy attacking all along the Regiment's front and infiltration into friendly positions, well behind the Main Line of Resistance. Wild fighting raged throughout the night and well into the next day as the fanatical attackers sought to break out into open country, but every measure was met by determined counterattacks. On the night of the 25th, the frustrated enemy fell back to his original line, leaving the ground littered with enemy dead. Despite the loss of 237 officers and men, the 222nd Infantry Regiment held its position, exacting a heavy toll of men and equipment from the enemy. The courage and devotion to duty shown by the members the 222nd Infantry Regiment in smashing one of the enemy's principal strategic efforts to reconquer Alsace, are worthy of emulation and exemplify the highest traditions of the Army of the United States.

CHAPTER NINE

MOYENVIC, FRANCE
RESERVE BASE
JANUARY 27, 1945

At last, the A/T Company was pulled together as a unit and were headed in convoys toward the rear echelon on our way to reserve base. Exhausted, GIs slept on the hard benches at the back of the trucks. Even with the jostling and bumpiness in the road, the dog-tired men kept sleeping. The convoy ended up at their assigned area for reserve base around noon the next day at a quaint little shelled-out village named Moyenvic. Upon arriving at the base, most everyone had to be shaken to wake up and be alert. Finally, we were at a place where we could rest, and to some degree, get a bit of peace and security.

As a unit, the A/T Company was exhausted, short of men, some were killed, wounded, and missing, and our equipment needed repair. We had been on the front lines for quite a while now, living and sleeping in the snow and muck. Our first order was to get cleaned up. Many of us hadn't had a bath in over a month and most of us had body lice (i.e. cooties!).

Having cooties to the extent they are in your eyebrows, nose and ears, not to mention other equally uncomfortable places, is something no one should ever have to experience in their lifetime. It is the ultimate misery a man can go through! There's no way you can forget their existence. Picking them off is a losing proposition because they multiply faster than you could remove them. Even under the rough circumstances we lived, it was no less embarrassing, and we tried to hide our suffering from each other. Dusting powder with an insecticide, also known as DDT, seemed to only feed the little critters giving way to a full-on attack. Gasoline rubdowns helped some, but created more problems than it solved. Have you ever tried washing woolen clothes with gasoline, then putting them on to wear? The idea that "cooties could rule the world" was the truth!

By the time we arrived at the reserve base, the Quartermaster Corps had the answer. To finally get rid of the lice, there was nothing left to do but have us remove (and burn) our clothes, line up, enter a dusting tent where we were fogged with DDT, take a shower (a wonderful and exhilarating hot shower), and then receive new clothes as we emerged at the other end of the shower tent. Degrading? Somewhat, but considerably more rewarding. Such sweet relief.

A LITTLE DECORATING DOESN'T HURT

The quarters that were assigned to squads were old and abandoned buildings in the business section of the small town of Moyenvic. As soon as we found our rooms, there were those, like myself, that collapsed as soon as we laid our head on a pillow; but some of the men started cleaning up and "redecorating" (I'm using the term loosely) to make our quarters seem a little more comfortable. Ingenious GIs used their talents to make a barren room look almost like home. Furniture miraculously appeared and stoves from "no one knows where" were installed. The GI decorators even hung draperies over a window or two. Pictures of wives and girlfriends were hung on the wall and the rooms became almost cozy - all the while we knew that it could be a matter of hours or days when we would get the call to head back to the front lines and have to abandon our newfound home.

It took us about three days to rest, get our quarters in shape, and get clean clothes and haircuts. During this period of rest and relaxation a dirty word was given as an order – training! This came as a shock to the men because they considered themselves battle-hardened and certainly didn't need any more training. It took some encouraging to convince my platoon that they just couldn't loaf for the time they were in the reserve base and still remain effective fighting men. To compromise, we did a little tweaking of the training schedule that allowed them to sneak off to an occasional movie or to get a travel pass.

Among the many well-organized and impressive arrangements planned by the Army, the base at Moyenvic offered a field movie theater, shower unit, library, PX, and other special services for the soldiers on reserve. An old barn was commandeered to be our theater with the latest releases we could view as many times as we wanted. On one occasion, we were watching a war movie with an artillery attack that was a little too realistic. The audience, including myself, couldn't get out of that barn soon enough! With all these indulgences, we slowly began to feel a little bit more human despite our training schedule from 6 am until way too late.

During my time off I would wander into the dorf of Moyenvic, where once again, I encountered the Red Cross. The polished and well equipped Red Cross vehicle was on the scene, attended by young and nice looking people serving coffee, doughnuts and cigarettes and charging too much for the meager salary the GIs received. At the same time back in the States, they were promoting that they were on the front lines even though they were far from it. Their photographers were told exactly what to film and at what angle to take the picture to make them look as good as possible. However, the more elderly Salvation Army staff passed out the same food and amenities but without charging a cent. They went about their services without any fanfare and working long hours with dedication. The latter certainly had the respect of the GIs who appreciated their loving kindness.

THE EXECUTION OF EDDIE SLOVIK

While in Moyenvic, I was called to the small commune of Sainte-Marie-Aux-Mines, about a two hour's drive south. It is here that a certain event happened. It is one in which I am haunted and conflicted about and have not spoken of. I was walking across a compound on the morning of January 31, when I remember being stopped by a captain that told me to follow him saying, "We need witnesses." I was led to a courtyard behind a home that was surrounded by a large wall and told I would be a witness to a military execution. As I watched, three soldiers proceeded to take Private Eddie Slovik up to a post that was standing in front of the wall and strip him of all his insignias and military identifications. He was then strapped to the post with belts.

The firing squad consisted of twelve soldiers. Customary of firing squads, out of the twelve rifles, eleven had a round of live ammunition and one was loaded with a blank. Upon the command of "FIRE!" the twelve soldiers fired at Eddie. I heard later that the eleven bullets that hit him didn't actually kill him at the moment, but by the time the soldiers reloaded, he had passed away. It was a terrible sight to witness for a twenty year old boy; and one I can never get out of my head, regardless of the reasons for the punishment.

Eddie Slovik had been court martialed in November 1944 for desertion and sentenced to a military execution. After the court martial, Private Slovik attempted to get leniency by writing a letter to General Eisenhower. His plea was denied. Desertion had become a problem in France and, in particular, during the Battle of the Bulge. Eisenhower made the decision that an example had to be made. Many soldiers during the course of the war had attempted to run away from the fight and were imprisoned – an outcome no doubt that Slovik had hoped for. Prior to the court Martial, he was given several chances to change his mind and return to his unit, but he insisted that given the chance again, he would run. Slovik thought that any punishment would be better than facing our foes in war. He had no idea that he would be the only soldier during World War II to be court martialed and executed for desertion.

I was there to witness it.

FIELD OF BODIES

It was not uncommon to come across displaced American or German war dead.

Upon our arrival in France we had learned of a historic event called the Malmedy Massacre, which occurred on December 17, 1944 in Belgium during the Battle of the Bulge. Eighty four US soldiers who had surrendered to the Germans were executed in a field. The discovery of this massacre would ripple through the chains of command, and orders were communicated down to the lowest levels to prevent US soldiers from retaliation.

Although not a massacre, the 2nd Platoon would encounter a similar wide open field littered with bodies. This field, free of trees, was the perfect place for the platoon to practice its infantry maneuvering exercises. As a few lead men, acting as points for the advancing unit, were moving out into the open field, they started stumbling in the three feet deep snow. At first they thought they were stumbling on fallen logs but on closer examination, these "logs" were the frozen bodies of fallen Germans from a previous battle.

The 2nd Platoon was then quickly pulled off the field and the findings were reported to Graves Registration who then took over the situation.

BACK TO THE FRONT

Just as we were getting into the swing of training with a degree of regularity, orders came for the division to move out and up into the front lines. We'd had our rest and now it was our turn to relieve the 179th Infantry Regiment of the 45th Division so they too might move into division reserve. All of the men's effort in changing our bunk into a home would now go to the next unit. We left everything as it was in hopes they would enjoy our redecorating!

CHAPTER TEN

VOSGES MOUNTAINS, FRANCE
FEBRUARY, 1945

We moved out of Moyenvic as a unit, joining the regimental convoy in the vicinity of Vic-sur-Seille, France. Together we moved northeast through the heavily wooded Forest Lorraine, a famous scene of Rainbow Division activity during World War I. Before the 179th Regiment left for reserve, the officers informed us of the situation and it was easy to see why they were in a big hurry to get the hell out of there. The change-over took place in the Vosges Mountains of France during the daylight hours making the process easier for us, but it also allowed the Germans to figure out what was taking place. Within moments of our exchange, German gunfire started bombarding our troops as we scrambled to get up to the MLR on top of a mountain ridge. It wasn't easy to climb up a passage there because the ground was partially frozen; but after a few passes of a truck, the ground became a muddy bog allowing us to continue navigating our way up the mountain.

Moving into a prepared MLR was considerably different than what we had previously been accustomed to. Foxholes and dugouts had already been established and were covered over by logs and three to four feet of snow and dirt. The 45th had been there for some time in a static position giving them plenty of opportunities to prepare their area to be as comfortable and as protective as possible. It was as if we exchanged our home at reserves for their home in a foxhole. Sensing we would be there for a time as well, troops began to make even more improvements by whatever means they could. After becoming accustomed to the situation and how the terrain lay, shifts were organized in manning our lines. Our hot meals were sent up twice a day and we ate our K-rations the rest of the time. Every two weeks the men were rotated back to Wingen-sur-Moder where there were field baths, movies, the Salvation Army canteen (the Red Cross was nowhere in sight), clean clothes and other conveniences. As we lay in our dugouts, we were pretty happy if we just had dry socks and an occasional change of underwear. Shaving became a passion since we had finally rid ourselves of lice in Moyenvic and didn't want give those little monsters a reason to stir up again.

The Germans, having occupied the area previously, had mined and booby trapped the woods making it an extremely dangerous area. Our dugouts were secure but once we stepped out of them it was a different matter. Although many of the mines had been located by the 179th troops, there were still several which remained active in the area. There were hundreds of schu-mine 42s, a small box-like device about the size of a box of kitchen matches, placed in the firebreaks and on trails in the woods. German patrols passing in front of and behind the lines would bury them in shallow holes, then camouflage them with leaves and twigs. They were a real menace for the GIs who could set one off merely by the pressure of his weight. It would maim him terribly as well as anyone near him at the time the mine was set off. Since they were so hard to detect, we considered them one of the worst of the mines. Then, there were the German stick grenades nicknamed "potato mashers". The potato masher was a grenade with a unique design. It sported a handle to make it easier to throw further. We also found these weapons tied to fine wires hanging from trees along our path ready to kill the unwary man who might move into the wire and trigger the grenade.

THE POWER OF THE AIR CORPS

At a time when we had relative quietness in our sector, the Air Corps offered an opportunity for an infantry officer to swap places with an Air Corps Officer in order to give both sides a perspective of their duties. Lieutenant John C. Bolt Jr., Mine Platoon leader, was given the first and only rotation. As it turned out, he was gone for five days. On returning, he gave a vivid description of the bombing raid he went on, stating unequivocally that he didn't mind forgoing the clean sheets, hot meals, Scotch whiskey and warm quarters the Air Corps enjoyed in order to keep his two feet on the ground. It might be noted that no Air Corps Officer showed up to replace Bolt in his absence, which left us one man short.

One of my more vivid memories is the sound of bombers coming over the lines at night. Some came from Italy and others from England and France. It would take thirty minutes to an hour for them to pass over on their way to the target, and more than two or three hours before they would return on their way back to base. On occasions, we saw them bombing nearby cities of Wissembourg, France and Worms, Germany. The sky would light up and the bombs could be heard and the earth shook. Although the sight of the Air Force bombers passing by us was always reassuring, their noise drowned out any chance of the GI hearing an incoming enemy patrol. The Germans were smart enough to take advantage of the situation and at times used those moments to successfully pass through our MLR and cause trouble for us.

By the beginning of March, the weather began to clear up, allowing American air cover to be even more effective. The Air Corps began a series of strafings from low flying aircraft. Sporadically, the division would be alerted to "watch our heads". We knew this meant the Air Corps would be conducting their strafings directly in front of our lines and every precaution had to be taken because of their proximity to our fronts. On occasion there were reports of rounds falling short in and behind our lines but not often. The sheer impact of these concentrated shellings were unbelievable in their intensity. Every GI at one time or another felt some pity for the poor Germans who bore the brunt of these saturations. The noise was deafening as the ground shook violently – every head was down in a foxhole or taking some form of cover. The Germans had their times of bombarding the Allies but none like the elevated intensity we gave to them. Concentrations of this scope by the Air Corps would undoubtedly leave the Germans reeling and in no condition to launch an attack. After such concentrations, their mortar rounds seemed like cap pistols.

A RESPITE WITH SWEET CREAM

As we marched on to move to another location, we came to a small dorf where a few brave inhabitants remained. As we walked through the dorf, we came across a business we hadn't seen before. A creamery operator had ignored the fact that his dorf was on the front line and had boldly continued to operate his business. Several of us went inside to investigate its contents, and there we saw it - a vat of raw, whole, refrigerated sweet milk! Having lived off powdered milk for so long, we would have gladly given the owner everything we had for a taste, however, with cigarettes and K-rations, we were able to help ourselves to the best milk we had ever tasted. The vat was some four feet lower when we got through drinking and had to leave it behind. What a sacrifice to leave all of that delicious milk to go off and fight a war!

A CHANGE OUT

The situation on the MLR had become somewhat routine. With the exception of patrols, holding the line was a daily pattern of rotation. As with any extended routine, the GIs became too comfortable and bad habits started to develop. We had experienced this before and, despite the warnings, recognized it as a bad situation. Carelessness would surely follow. Whether this was the reason or not, the 222nd was relieved by the 242nd on March 11th and 12th – a welcome change. The long, bitterly cold days and nights had taken its toll on the men. While casualties had been relatively low, there were frazzled nerves aggravated by the time the men spent waiting – waiting for relief, waiting until dark when there was hope for a hot meal, waiting to take care of ordinary functions, waiting for mail, and waiting for a rotation.

During our time to prepare for the change out, there were heavy artillery exchanges and activity. What a relief when the heavenly order to change out with units of the 242nd began to take place. The 222nd wanted to get back behind the lines before the Germans suspected what was happening. Later, some of the men of the 222nd had lots of laughs saying the Krauts were probably the ones ordering our being replaced! They shelled intermittently during the two days it took to pull out, making the change-out more or less a nightmare. Moving during the night with the mortars aimed on us caused substantial damage with more casualties and greater confusion than had been expected.

After the change-out, we relocated to a small village called Puberg, located between Wingen-sur-Moder and Sarre-Union. The units were scattered around the village and the platoons were given instructions for deployment in case of attacks and needing to move out. It was here that I had one of the more traumatic experiences of my service.

One murky night, while walking through Puberg to check on my platoon, I rounded the corner of a building and was confronted by the figure of a German soldier holding a machine gun directly at my face. With thoughts tumbling through my mind, I realized there was nothing I could do but drop to the frozen ground with the faint hope of missing the slaughter that was sure to come. But then, just as suddenly, I recognized that there was something unusual about the soldier. There was no gun going off and no movement. Regaining my senses from complete terror, I came to realize that the German who was manning the machine gun was dead. He was in a position in which he could easily have fired the gun, but he had received a bullet between his eyes and was frozen into position.

I disarmed and repositioned the body of the German soldier so that no one would find themselves in the same circumstance. Although I was shaking from the exhilaration of the moment, I went on to my duties. Afterwards, I awoke many nights sweating out that moment, seeing the German's eyes, frozen expression, and the machine gun at my face. A horrible memory.

Division reserve was different this time from what we had previously experienced. Instead of resting and regrouping, we had to be on constant alert. The Germans were expected to make pincer attacks – this is when military forces simultaneously attack both sides of the lines at one time. They had done this same attack in the Battle of the Bulge, cutting off our thinly manned front lines. It was a time for high security and officers had to attend briefings two to four times a day. Still, our lives here were better than the bitter cold and wet woods on the MLR.

This time for our housing while in reserve, instead of being put up in empty buildings, soldiers went through the town and took over warm, dry houses where we could clean ourselves up, clean our weapons, and sleep continuously for the four hour shifts we took off from guard duty. As the Army would have it, before everyone got their places located, more training was announced. Would there be no end to it?

Mercifully, most of the training was out of the cold and wet and was centered on mountain tactics – a completely new subject to the A/Ters. We did lots of reviewing of the disarming of anti-personnel mines and focused heavily on detecting booby traps. The bazookas that the 2nd had requisitioned were given out and the ammunition for them was supplemented. And, as it so happened, we learned of a new kind of comrade who would fight by our sides - Army mules!

Large mules were issued to the units along with a mule skinner, something new for most of us. The mule skinner's sole purpose was to keep the mules moving. GIs practiced loading ammunition on a mule, removing it, and learning how to care for them. They were contrary beasts! We knew the mules would be carrying supplies up the mountain for us, but at the time, we didn't realize how important they would be in fulfilling our mission. One of our naive GIs, who had been assigned a mule, took it into his quarters when he had been told that they would be "sleeping with them." He never outlived that moment when we pushed them both out on the street!

CHAPTER ELEVEN

OPERATION UNDERTONE
HARDT MOUNTAINS/SIEGFRIED LINE
MARCH 15TH, 1945

On the morning of March 14th, orders thundered - "Jump off at 0400 March 15th, Siegfried Line to be breached!" The alarming order only amplified the seriousness of the situation with the advancing German forces - the next big challenge for the Rainbow Division. We quickly scattered to make our plans for securing proper equipment and munitions to accompany the troops. We looked to find safe parking for the 57mm guns, figured how to get one or more bazooka rounds on a mule, wrote one more letter home, looked for one more "coke in a green bottle", and stowed our personal items on the trucks for safe keeping.

I received a briefing and the maps which covered the anticipated routes of our mission. As our troops made preparations, Sgt. Geary and I studied the information with the squad leaders until we memorized each detail. We learned that the Germans were shaping up to attack the front of the 232nd MLR. We altered our plans time and time again to adjust to any movement or new information as it came in. I'm not sure how we were able to keep up with all the details before the time came to depart from Puberg, France. Once we did, it didn't take long for our previous orderliness to erupt into total disorder! Most troops became confused trying to keep up with assigned units and they scrambled to find their placements, all the while handling the cantankerous mules.

It was important to remain as quiet as possible as we readied ourselves for the move but those damned mules brayed like fog horns sounding off. If the Germans didn't suspect what was happening, they were either deaf or from another world! Finally, 0430 came and the Anti-Tankers moved out toward our ordered Point of Departure (POD) - a paved road running roughly northwest to southeast meandering through the mountains between Rothbach, France and Sägmühle, Germany. There was a creek on one side of the road, fortunately not wide, nor deep; and, on the other side were mountains, not hills mind you - but steep, wooded, rocky mountains. When the A/Ters reached the POD around 0600, 1st Battalion had already crossed the creek and were climbing the mountain. No resistance…yet. After we threaded across the creek and began the ascent of the mountain with the mules braying in harmony, some mortars began to fire on the road causing us to proceed more cautiously. The forward movement was slow as we waited on the point troops to clear out any enemy activity and entrenchments along the ridge line of the mountain to the northeast.

About 0800, the situation changed dramatically. Mortars and artillery erupted along the ridgeline and the valley below. The nonstop firing was "walking" up and down the valley floor, ridgeline, and mountain side indiscriminately. Its intensity increased until around 1000 when the forward troops were stopped by a solid line of enemy resistance. All hell broke loose as short trajectory shells seemed to strike almost every tree around us, causing bursts of branches and showers of leaves to rain down on the GIs causing chaos and casualties. We were hit continuously by enemy snipers and rifle troops at the same time as what seemed liked hundreds of wired grenades and Shu-mine were set off. A squad from our Mine Platoon passed through our lines to go before us to disarm the Schu-mines, but many of the mules had discovered the mine field first.

No description is adequate to describe the screaming of the mules that had been wounded. The sound they made was much like that of a woman's scream - high pitched, ear piercing, and blood curdling! They were running wildly through the woods with their entrails hanging outside their bodies as they shrieked. Their assigned GI had either been killed, wounded, or lost the reins. The horrific sounds carried through the woods mingling with the explosions of the never-ending gunfire. Shrapnel ricocheted off of trees and rocks like missiles. The overwhelmed GIs weren't able to tell which direction the shots were coming from. Where were the machine guns? Where were the snipers? It was a time of utter chaos.

Through the chaos, Captain Lummus gave new orders to 2nd Platoon, moving us into a position on the south side of the mountain, about halfway up from the valley floor. The continuing tree bursts kept any movement from being fast or rash. There wasn't time for digging foxholes but only enough time for getting behind trees and hoping it wasn't the next tree to explode. German snipers were camouflaged in such a way that they were never spotted, their efforts were devastating – morally and physically. Forward movement began again around 1400 after it was reported that B Company had cleaned out the machine gun nest which had stopped our progress. This slow and deliberate movement forward was again stopped a short time later by what appeared to be a German Final Protective Line (FPL) with two machine guns. In the dense woods, it was inconceivable that the Germans were able to find a line of sight of any distance for their FPL– but it happened. Lummus ordered 1st Platoon to neutralize the machine gun on the right flank and down toward the valley floor. 2nd (my platoon) was to move forward and fill in the gap, keeping contact with 1st Platoon on the right and with 3rd Platoon on the left. Rifle fire came from dug-in Krauts – seemingly everywhere and all at the same time.

For some hour or more, the enemy machine guns and rifle troops kept everyone pinned down with nothing more than ricochets. Then the

German artillery and mortars began coming in more heavily, walking up and down the ridge line with murderous tree bursts. Lummus gave me orders to take some men and check on what was happening to 1st Platoon (their radio was out), and to help them silence the German's machine gun that was holding the line. I took four men with a bazooka and moved over toward A Company's 1st Platoon. Movement was slow with wounded GIs in our path reaching out for help in getting a medic, but the continuous artillery and mortar barrages kept medics from being able to get anywhere near the wounded men laying scattered on the forest floor.

At some point, I decided to shoot a bazooka through a clearing in the trees hoping to hit near the nest of a German unit (the exact location couldn't be determined even at this point of proximity) and at least get the attention of the machine gunner and his outposts. Just as the shot was about to fire, an artillery barrage came in. All I can remember is a loud, powerful explosion, blinding light, a tree blasting into a thousand pieces, and then everything going dark. This time the tree burst had hit its mark.

Upon regaining my senses, I found myself laying at the base of a tree which was situated between me and the enemy lines. Hoping I was just numb from the hit and would be up in time to move on and fire the bazooka at my target, I tried to move up on my elbows but fell back to the ground. With that, my mind went quickly to check my injuries. My head could turn slightly from side to side but it took considerable effort and the pain was horrendous. I tried to move my legs, but couldn't, and found I was only capable of scooting my body forward, if I had wanted to move at all. It was then that I knew I had been hit and had a degree of shell shock. Unknown to me, in my absence, Sergeant Geary had taken command of my platoon and had moved on to attack.

After a time laying in the snow trying to gain some sense of what had happened, I heard some heavy breathing and movement, then realized that I wasn't completely alone. Another wounded soldier lay about thirty feet from me, also in a prone position. I asked if I could help him, but only heard his groans. Although I couldn't fully get up, I was able to crawl over to him inching my way on my elbows. Again, I asked if I could help him, he responded that he just needed to rest for a few minutes and then he would get up and help me. On looking closer, I saw that the man's body was cut nearly half in two, probably from a direct hit. What kept the man alive, bleeding as profusely as he was, is a mystery. We talked a bit as best we could and he was somewhat coherent. It turned out that although I hadn't seen him since OCS, he was one of my classmates at A&M. We had graduated from the same class and he had gone on to be a forward observer with a chemical mortar battalion. As he slowly fell silent, he whispered for his mother until the moment he died. It was an honor to have had a few moments with that brave GI, and something died in me as I watched him take his last breath.

Drifting in and out of consciousness, I began to relive the deafening explosion, the acrid smell of smoke and the shaking of the ground, all the while the sky was growing dark and the air was getting colder. My calls for a medic went unanswered. As I remember it, at around 2000 hours I became aware of my surroundings and saw Geary by my side - greeting me with that cocky side grin and welcoming me back to consciousness. In a more serious tone he told me he couldn't move me with the injury I had sustained and that he was going to get a medic. I lay there all night, passing in and out of reality, hearing the sounds of troop movement, hearing wounded mules scream and the blasts from the occasional artillery barrages. The cold didn't seem to bother me although the temperature must have dropped below freezing that night. The only thing I could remember was saying "Don't worry, Mama".

In the early morning hours I recognized the pain from my rib cage as if my heart was hurting with each throb. Soon after daylight, a medic found me and immediately began to administer morphine. Thankfully, the medicine knocked me out completely until stretcher bearers came to pick me up and hoist me onto a stretcher. Having been working nonstop for days, the poor bearers were worn out and had to be relieved several times to carry me through the rough mountainous terrain. The first thing I remembered after receiving the morphine was when the bearers stumbled on the rocky hillside, dropping the stretcher and dumping me on the ground. The horrific pain of that moment kept me awake and aware of the heavy load I must have been for the men – all this as I heard the "walking" up and down of artillery on the ridge in the background.

Along the way, as they carried me from the front lines to the rear, we passed Lieutenant Colonel Lucien E. Bolduc, deputy commander of the 222nd, who would later become commander in April, who noted that I was being carried on the stretcher with my hands on my head – the usual position that German soldiers had as a sign of surrender. For a brief moment, I remember him chuckling at my position, declaring I was NOT a prisoner, and several of the soldiers watching me and yelling out a "hur –rah" as I went through the woods. The stretcher bearers must have carried me two to four miles over the mountain before getting to a battalion aid station. Once at the station, Major Joseph P. Shelc, who was the regimental surgeon, asked if I wanted another shot of morphine – but not knowing how long it had been since I had received the last one, he made the decision not to give me another one.

At this point I was loaded into an ambulance for the trip to a field hospital. The ambulance, equipped to carry seven men, was loaded with ten GIs. Because of the rough terrain, the driver couldn't help but hit bump after agonizing bump, keeping me from passing out as the pain was torturing me. I was somewhat relieved that my wounds weren't as serious as some of the other fellows on the trip. I heard their deep moaning and murmurings, wondering if they too would make it out alive. During the trip, the soldier laying above me started hemorrhaging and the blood spilled over onto me, I couldn't move so I just laid on the cot as the blood trickled onto me. But even at that time, you couldn't tell whose blood was whose. I spent that painful trip wondering what had happened to me. What had hit me? Where was I wounded, how serious was it, why couldn't I move my arms and legs? I was terrified.

After I arrived at the 95th Evacuation Hospital, doctors told me that shrapnel had lodged into my back close to my spine and I needed immediate surgery to avoid any life-threatening consequences. They put me under sedation and I can't remember anything more than the scurrying around of all the medical personnel. One doctor's facial expression haunted me for a long time afterwards because even out of his apparent fatigue, he showed concern for my condition. They cleaned me up and filled me with morphine before I was transferred to the 23rd General Hospital at Vittel, France. Mercifully, I have no memories of that ride.

After arriving at the hospital, I was operated on immediately. The tree burst that had caused my wound had sent shrapnel dangerously close to my spine. My first recollection as I became conscious was the warm feeling in my body as I woke in a nice hospital room with clean sheets, pleasant surroundings, and with a sense of peace and security. As I looked around the room, I had the distinct feeling that I had died and gone to heaven but I just couldn't rationalize the bed pan being thrust under me as being very heavenly!

The hospital at Vittel was one of the most unusual places I've ever been. It was a private estate before being taken over by the Army. There were over one hundred and twenty bedrooms in the estate with all of the necessary facilities making it a ready-made hospital. The manicured grounds were landscaped as if on a picture postcard. It was a magnificent home with grand architecture. The ceiling in my bedroom had one of the most beautiful pieces of art painted on it that I've ever seen; and I had plenty of time to study it while lying on my back.

My recuperation began immediately. While being kept in a degree of sedation, I was given physical therapy twice daily, starting the day after my operation. A massage under heat lamps, with oil and the experienced fingers of a nurse would lull me to sleep after stretching exercises (painful to say the very least). On the second or third day she would deftly flick a scab from the wound on my back with her finger nail – oh, if I could have only had the energy to scream from the pain! This torture continued each day during my stay in the hospital as the nurse lulled me into a dreamlike state, then giving a "flick" to an errant scab. Later, as the sedation had worn off and the pain medication ended, she encouraged conversation with me as if I was talking to her like a brother. The sole purpose of her camaraderie was to speed up my recovery so as to help me return to my troops. Cruel, but effective.

To be completely honest, all of my time at the hospital wasn't just misery and suffering. After a bit of time in recovery, I was placed in a ward with seven other officers - each having varying injuries or conditions. One day a young lady – very attractive in a sexy way, obviously French with heavy make-up and dressed to kill, came into our room "peddling her wares". A colonel across from me, having been away from home for some time, and for obvious reasons, decided to "buy" her. After retreating to the bathroom with the mademoiselle, it was only a few minutes when an uproar of laughter came from the bathroom and out bolted the outraged colonel. The tasty dish turned out to be an enlisted male patient from down the hall who had fixed up for the joke. Only minutes earlier, an anticipating horde of men had burst into the bathroom to expose the hoax. It was a great diversion for us, but the colonel didn't take it very well and he immediately requested a change of scenery.

Numerous jokes and entertainment were always available from the patients. I learned that, unbeknownst to me, a quart of whiskey taken from my belongings had contributed to getting these shenanigans pulled off! Fortunately, I was spared being the butt of one of their jokes but always enjoyed the fun. Another situation I remember was of a young officer in the ward who had found it necessary to have a circumcision during his service overseas (not uncommon at the time). While he was recuperating, a beautiful young nurse, who looked like a movie star (it seemed they all did), would come to his bedside for therapy. She would softly talk to him at the same time rubbing the inner part of his leg. Even the statue of David would have been excited! The resulting pain caused screams from both anguish and pain!

But all was not perfect. My concern, "Don't worry, Mama!", had not been unfounded. She would soon receive the dreaded MIA (Missing in Action) notice. Soon afterward the MIA notice was changed to a KIA (Killed in Action) notice. Against Army policy, these letters reached them before they received the correction of my being WIA (Wounded in Action). My family was damaged that day after reading the notices and I considered the two errors as being inexcusable. My parents, especially my mother, suffered terribly by their mistake.

My therapy continued for about six weeks, but contrary to medical advice, I was "pushed" toward a complete recovery. My youth helped the speedy recovery and since my wound wasn't considered the worst of what wartime brought, I was released too soon for the journey back to join my troops. I had been keeping in touch with developments on a daily basis and was eager to rejoin my fellow officers and men, but I was filled with questions. What will the situation be once I get back to the company? Will I be able to perform as an officer with my wounds? Will I be able to face the same situations again?

AWARD OF BRONZE STAR MEDAL

While moving forward to investigate enemy activity on Hill 409 during the general offensive through the Hardt Mountains, Lieutenant Westbrook was seriously wounded by devastating mortar and artillery fire. Refusing to be evacuated by litter bearers until his wounded men had been cared for, he attempted to make his way through the deadly barrage to safety but collapsed from his wounds and weakened condition. Through his outstanding courage and heroic devotion to his men, Lieutenant Westbrook was an inspiration to the attacking riflemen. Entered military service from Rule, Texas.

CHAPTER TWELVE

RETURNING TO THE FRONT
APRIL 1945

I hitchhiked a ride with standard Army jeeps and fast-tracked my way back to home base on April 23, 1945. The trip back, like my recuperation, was hurried and seemed like a record trip for the Army. Because of my weakened condition, the truck rides, the tent cities, and more truck rides, took a toll on my body. I was weak, at times dizzy, and extremely sore. There's no question that I returned too soon after my wound. Fortunately, my company commander Captain Jack Edling and Sergeant Geary could easily see my condition and relieved me for a spell during my more physical duties until I had adequately recovered.

During my absence I had been replaced temporarily and upon returning was assigned to a liaison capacity. Nonetheless, I was drawn to my old platoon and hopeful of getting back to being its leader. It seemed that my injury was behind me and the whole future was mine. I knew I wasn't immortal, but at the time I felt I was damned near it, and tried my best to keep up with my responsibilities.

Elements of the A/T Company were now located at Gunzenhausen, Germany, south of Nuremberg, and were still smarting from the taking of the dorf of Furth, Germany, which had been one of the severest battles for them. The regiment had just been relieved by the 242nd and had been sent to division reserve - eager to find a place to pause, lick wounds, recoup, regroup, and get ready to re-enter the chase. Geary, who had taken over for me during my absence, was more than happy to turn the command back to me. It was depressing to see the state of the division. Their faces, bodies and morale showed the hard times from the battles at Furth. They had endured the fatigue, grime, loss of equipment, and worse - the loss of men. With little time to catch up, we were at division reserve for only a few days before we had to be on the move again.

On April 27th, we left the division reserve base and moved toward the frontal action near the dorf of Holzheim, Germany. The 45th Division was on the left of the 42nd and the 36th Division was on its right flank. For reasons I didn't understand, while I was in the hospital the communication and cooperation between the 42nd and the 45th broke down and became even problematic at times. This failing continued for some time and sadly resulted in future problems.

On our march north, we found resistance in every dorf and encountered endless roadblocks that had been set up by the Germans. We bypassed most of the roadblocks so we wouldn't have to slow down the momentum of our advance. There was no question that our air superiority was the backbone of the advance, and air strikes were called upon regularly to neutralize the resistance we encountered. At this point we were moving only four to seven miles a day.

On the road to Holzheim, we met major points of resistance with German troops consisting of SS and Wehrmacht insiders; and at times, had to call upon artillery to support our advance. During one of our battles, the 222nd regiment faced the horrific German 88mm field pieces in low trajectory fire, and it was a demoralizing situation. With time, our artillery put the 88mms out of action but not without a high cost to human life. While the situation has been described as "routine action" in accounts, the GIs who were doing the routines didn't consider it as such. Some ground was gained but we had suffered many wounded and far too many dead.

That night there was little rest. Troops would stop at their intended objective, establish perimeter security, and dig-in to collect themselves. Patrols were sent out to secure information on the enemy and, if possible, provide intelligence for the next day's operations. The patrols were on the order of combat patrols, and they made contact regularly with enemy installations. The next morning the attack was on again and based on the information gathered from the previous night's patrol, the German installations were destroyed.

I was reeling with the effects of my injury. The pain, weakness, and shock from my wound made it difficult for me to keep pace. At times medics had to rush in to handle the hemorrhaging of my wound but I carried on and it didn't stop me from my duties. The men who had suffered under my super-stamina during calisthenics months back at Camp Gruber, now enjoyed kidding me about "having me right where they wanted me!" The rest I longed for wasn't possible and sleep came only in catnaps when and where they could be stolen.

1LT Jack Westbrook
© Westbrook Archive

Fort McClellan, Alabama. Basic Infantry Training.
Jack is on the far left, top row.
© Westbrook Archive

Camp Gruber. Jack inspecting 2nd
Platoon. © Westbrook Archive

Camp Gruber. Jack is in the front, 2nd Platoon stands at attention behind him. © Westbrook Archive

Camp Gruber. Jack is on the far right with the men of 2nd Platoon on a training exercise. © Westbrook Archive

TSGT Joseph B. Geary

New York City, Cafe Zanzibar, November 1944. Far left, Jack. Far right, 1LT Russel Fielding. © Westbrook Archive

CP2, France. Chow line on 13 December 1944. Jack labeled this photo TSGT Hugh Brown, SGT Geary, SGT Doyle, PFC Stone, Unidentified. © Westbrook Archive

This 42nd Division photo of unidentified men in unidentified company and regiment shows the scope of the tent city at CP2.
© *Pathfinder Research Archive*

SSG Ivan M. Jones,
aka SGT Kilroy

The original message SGT Geary sent to HQ on 25 January, 1945
© *Westbrook Archive*

France, 1945. PFC James L. Hale, PFC James R. Morgan, PFC Russel L. Wolfe, PFC Kenneth A. Del Greco, PFC Julian H. Corbett, PFC Louis J. Cozic, PFC William J. Kluck, with Anti-Tank Company Truck #9. © Pathfinder Research Archive

A drawing of Jack by PFC Joseph P. Pocrnich. © Westbrook Archive

Moyenvic, France. February 1945. Top row: SSG Thomas M. Hess, PFC James R. Morgan, SSG Ivan M. Jones, TEC5 William C. DeGroot, TSGT Glen D. Dix, PFC Longin P. Bielan. Bottom row: SGT Pasquale E. Morone, PFC John D. Rennick, SSG Michael Spanish, PFC William E. Iverson. © Pathfinder Research Archive

110 • JACK E. WESTBROOK

Wingen sur Moder, February 1945. SSG Ivan M. Jones, 1LT Jack E. Westbrook, PFC Longin P. Bielan, PFC John D. Rennick, PFC William E. Iverson, SSG Thomas M. Hess, PFC James R. Morgan, SSG Michael Spanish, TSGT Glen D. Dix. © Pathfinder Research Archive

Hospital in Vittel, France, March 1945. © Westbrook Archive

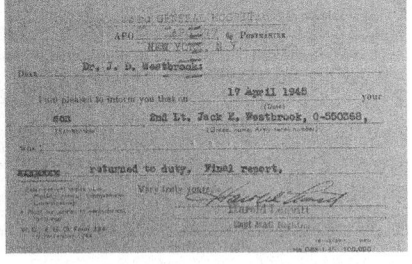

Jack has returned to duty after a stay in the 23rd General Hospital. © Westbrook Archive

Jack captioned this photo: Our quarters in the lumber miller's home. May 15, 1945. Schwent, Austria. © Westbrook Archive

Jack captioned this photo: This is the home that we are staying in. May 23, 1945. Theirsee, Austria. © Westbrook Archive

Jack captioned this photo: Davis just couldn't imagine that there was this much money. Monastery in Austria after the silver was found, July 1945. © Westbrook Archive

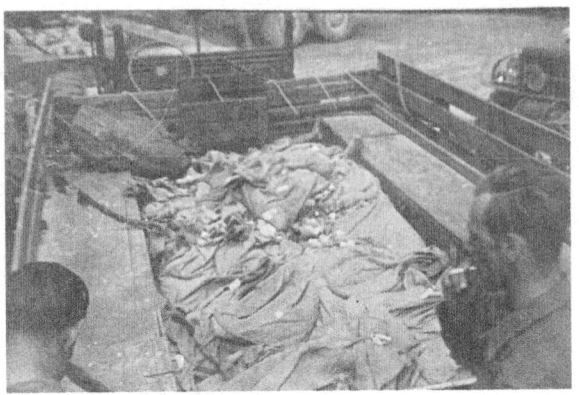

Jack captioned this photo: SSG William J. Kluck and PFC James L. Hale, google-eyed, look over the gelt. Monastery after the silver was found, July 1945. Austria.
© *Westbrook Archive*

The trucks leaving the monastery with the silver, on their way to deliver it to Salzburg, Austria.
© *Westbrook Archive*

A cancelled silver coin found in Austria
© *Westbrook Archive*

1LT Jack Westbrook in Schwaz, Austria. July 1945.
© Westbrook Archive

1LT Jack Westbrook. Jack captioned this photo: Ready to take off for Salzburg for the festival. July 1945.
© Westbrook Archive

Jack captioned this photo: Doc Horten, T-4 Blister Specialist. Morzg, Austria. August 1945.
© Westbrook Archive

Jack and PFC John J. Nonamaker on their way to Italy.
© Westbrook Archive

1LT Jack Westbrook, possibly in Italy, 1945.
© Westbrook Archive

WESTBROOK BOYS MEET IN ITALY

Dr. and Mrs. J. D. Westbrook received a telephone call Tues. from their sons Jiggs and Jack from Italy. Jiggs is stationed near there and Jack is in Austria but obtained leave and is visiting his brother and the 2 are celebrating and sight seeing in Italy. According to reports they are having a grand time together for their first time since Christmas 1942 when they both visited their parents at Rule.

The news of the Westbrook boys' reunion made the local paper.
© Westbrook Archive

Jack in Vienna, at the Sass home.
© Westbrook Archive

Papa Sass, Vienna, 1945.
© Westbrook Archive

Papa and Mama Sass,
Vienna 1945.
© Westbrook Archive

The Sass family sent Jack
their china after he returned
home to the States.
© Westbrook Archive

Marine barracks beside the Danube in Linz, Austria that became the CP for the company.
© Pathfinder Research Archive

2LT John C. Bolt
© Westbrook Archive

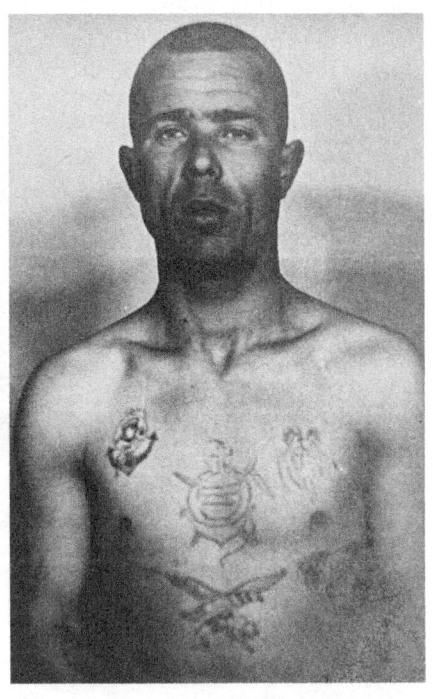

Jack captioned this:
The one and only Stoop - the original.
My Russian Comrade, Urfahr Bridge,
Linz. March 1946.
© Westbrook Archive

PART III: DACHAU

CHAPTER THIRTEEN

LIBERATION OF DACHAU
APRIL 29, 1945

In our briefing at Holzheim, we were told there was an encampment of importance north of Munich, Germany but nothing more was said to the troops of what was in store for us. There was no information as to location, size of the encampment or what actions we were to take, nor any plans on how to handle the inmates. We assumed that it would be another small labor camp of one hundred to one hundred and fifty people and would not involve the Rainbow Division other than for a short security job.

Previously, we had gone into areas where prisoners were being held as laborers. We saw the sordid conditions in which the Poles, Hungarians, Czechs, Germans, and other nationalities were being held. "Displaced Persons", or DPs as they were called, had been imprisoned and were worked and mistreated in appalling ways. They were forced to live in squalid conditions with little food and were worked from dawn to night and beaten if they didn't comply. Upon our arrival, we would interrogate many of these prisoners, and with the information they gave to us we were able to flush out many of our enemies.

It was both interesting and ironic to see the belligerence of the prisoners in their reaction to being freed and finally having the opportunity to express their rage toward their German captors.

With their anger and hostility, the DPs became such a problem and so dangerous to their German captors that many of them had to be restrained and placed in custody. They didn't take this kindly and under the circumstances, it seemed cruel. Still, it was a necessary step in order to protect the German captives. We were bound by the Geneva Convention, as well as for humane reasons, to protect even the foulest of our prisoners. In return, the DPs were highly indignant, cursing the American soldiers as being as bad as the Nazis. In time, it became easier for us to simply segregate, feed, and corral them in much the same way as their former captors.

With this as our background, nothing could have prepared American soldiers for what they witnessed on April 29, 1945 when they came to the concentration camp at Dachau. Little did anyone know that what they were about to see would stay with them for the rest of their lives.

The camp was located about fifteen miles northwest of Munich, and built on the edge of the town of Dachau - population of about ten thousand at the time. Our reconnaissance troops and point units got to the eastern side of the camp first. With just one look, they knew we had nowhere near the strength to deal with the situation. This was new ground for the American troops and we were concerned with how to handle it. There were so many questions. The 42nd Division didn't want to walk into a situation they were unfamiliar with, and they didn't want the prisoners of the camp to get caught in crossfire between the Germans and the Americans. Mainly, as I remember from my vantage point, the division was afraid of a trap being set by the Germans to lure us into the camp and then use the prisoners as shields. There was also a question of security around the perimeter of the camp. How do we prevent the German troops from entering the camp from a blind side and how do we prevent German troops that are inside the camp from escaping? Ironically, with all these other problems, we found that what we really needed was security to keep the prisoners from running rampant out of the compound and overrunning the countryside.

The 42nd Division went into the eastern side of the compound. At the time, we had no idea how large or far the camp extended. We learned afterwards that the 45th Division entered the western part of the concentration camp at about the same time. The camp was surrounded by an electrified fence and a moat. As a map later indicated, the section for the prisoners was approximately five acres and a much larger section, which included SS barracks, factories, an SS training school and administrative offices, covered about twenty acres. Several divisions of the camp were sectioned off in order to maintain security, control, and to segregate the inmates. A rail siding of eight tracks serviced the camp and was separated by fencing. The quarters in which the inmates existed were barrack-type buildings and service buildings that looked more like sheds than buildings. Another section of the camp was for the "bath" (gas) house, the ovens, and other service facilities used in the extermination process. There were found several facilities in which the inmates had been used in cruel medical and military experiments. There wasn't coal to use in the cremation process at the time so the ovens were cool; yet there were stacks of bodies outside the crematorium as well as inside the ovens waiting to be cremated. The stench of the sweet odor of burned and decayed human flesh still hung over the camp's ovens. At some time before the 42nd reached the camp, the Germans marched several thousand of the healthier inmates southeast of the town of Dachau to keep them out of the hands of the Americans. Later these inmates were found and held by the GIs.

As troops approached the compound, they didn't know whether the perimeter fence was still electrified. To their horror, soldiers saw internees running to greet them. Perhaps they mistakenly believed the fence was no longer charged. Or, perhaps in their exuberance and the chaos of the situation they overlooked the fact. They threw themselves against the fence, and were electrocuted immediately. Somehow the prisoners opened the gates to allow the troops to enter. There were still guards armed with machine guns in towers at vantage points but soldiers were able to overtake them immediately by either taking them as prisoners or by shooting and killing the more hostile guards. Inside, a few remaining SS soldiers were found with large and fierce German Shepherd dogs patrolling among the buildings and internees. Noticeably, most of the SS had fled by the time GIs came to the compound. The Americans advanced cautiously to ensure they weren't walking into a trap.

Behind the gates, the prisoners were in every state of malnutrition. They were partially clothed in rags, and infested with lice and other vermin. The majority of the inmates were old, diseased, crippled, and incapable of being of any physical use to the Germans. There were many children, but they too were crippled and diseased with no future of being used by their captors. As troops entered the compound, many of the captives were so decimated and near death that the mere excitement of being liberated caused their death. Fellow inmates listlessly carried about the sick and the bodies of those who had just expired, crying for the American doctors to bring them back to life. GIs openly wept as they saw the conditions these poor people lived in.

You must realize that there were over thirty two thousand detainees in the compound crowded into an area that would have been expected to hold less than three thousand. You could smell the stench of the camp several miles before it even came into sight, and it became overpowering by the time our troops came to the enclosure. The stink of the masses of bodies and the unsanitary conditions caused several soldiers, including myself, to vomit.

Immediately upon them entering the compound, hordes of the victims ran to the soldiers pleading for food and just as immediately, their pleas were answered by the GIs who gave them the K-rations they carried in their packs. Their rush for some sort of substance was short-lived as they choked down the rations; most of them vomited as soon as they swallowed the rich food. And yet, as they vomited, they scooped the bile up to try and eat it again. Their hunger was indescribable. GIs hurriedly pulled out blankets and clothing out of their packs and distributed them as fast as they could. We learned later that the internees were relieved to find that it was the Americans, not the Russians, who were their liberators. Having known the Russians and their appetite for cruelty, they had feared the possibility of the Russians reaching them first.

It was a difficult job to contain the milling throng of these poor human beings and establish any semblance of order. Amazingly, in spite of their frailty, many of the more capable prisoners wanted revenge. For people who were so malnourished and decimated, they came to have superhuman strength for the few moments that it took them to commit their own atrocities. These were instances that happened so fast, and in such volume, that we couldn't stop the inmates from their retribution as they pounced on their former captors.

As a result of what they had seen of the German inhumanity, the GIs couldn't help but pause hesitantly and wonder whether or not to let the inmates have their revenge. Some of the prisoners were wounded by the recklessness of their fellow inmates while showing their hatred towards the SS. The growing madness wasn't allowed to persist because of the insanity that was infecting them from their new found liberation. In the end, they had to be held and restrained; it wasn't practical to turn thirty two thousand ill, infested, and such-minded people loose on the countryside and on the German population.

It was customary for the AMG (American Military Government) officials, trained in establishing civilian order, to appear at every dorf, factory, or other establishment of any military significance. As an essential part of the liberation, they knew the layout of the camp, the town of Dachau, and they knew the officials and whether they could be trusted. I was amazed that the US and our Allies had planned so very well and to this extent. The specialists swarmed into the compound giving immediate medical aid, organizing the prisoners, and sealing off parts of the camp from both the prisoners and the GIs.

On the day of the liberation, I was still acting in a liaison capacity after being wounded, and was stationed about ¼ mile from the camp at the time the 42nd entered Dachau. The company commander gave me orders to locate Lieutenant Colonel Donald E. Downard, who had previously entered Dachau, and to get orders on our next set of movements. I jumped in my jeep and headed toward the only evident entry to the camp. Having heard shots being fired as I approached the compound, I was concerned as to what I might be getting into and was cautious. Because there was considerable concern about counterattacks by German tanks, Americans placed guns in defensive positions just east of the camp. As I drove closer to the camp, I spotted civilians from the town of Dachau riding their bicycles down the street in front of the entryway to the camp. Rags were tied over their noses and mouths to keep out the stench. Some of these same people later told us they didn't know what was going on in the camp, one of the most deliberate and ridiculous lies ever devised.

As I drove my jeep down the long boulevard to the camp, lined with beautiful trees and flowers, I came upon a picturesque entry with an elaborate wrought iron gate. In another day and time, I would have thought I was driving up to a girls' boarding school. Just before I got to the entryway, I recognized what the situation must have been and asked the American guards, who were now controlling the entrance, specifically of Downard's whereabouts. They didn't know his location at the time so I proceeded to go forward and look for myself. After I parked my jeep and walked to the main gate, I identified myself to the attending guards, explained my mission, and was permitted to enter the camp. Immediately, the atmosphere changed to one of disbelief and the incredible irony going from the rather magnificent entryway into a haunting, ghastly atmosphere.

I hadn't recognized the stench which had become pronounced a good distance from the installation, but upon entering the camp I came to realize it was the smell of death. As I recall, the time must have been after 2:00 pm. I assumed that the soldiers in charge of the situation were from the 42nd Rainbow Division, but I later found out that some of them were members of the 45th Division who had entered from a different location on or about the same time as the 42nd.

It was in my search for Downard that the true horrors of what had been happening at the camp opened up to me. There is no description adequate to completely picture what the situation was at Dachau. I witnessed a mass of humanity in their tattered and unkempt, filthy garb, with skin hanging from their bones. They stared from hollow eyes that seemed to sink into their skeletal faces, crying and screaming as they reached through the fence seemingly only wanting to touch me. Their look encompassed the emotions of despair, hopelessness, confusion, defeat, nothingness – they were all lost souls. Nothing more could happen to them that would shock them, pain them, or surprise them. They were at the end of their sanity as they existed under impossible circumstances and conditions. And now they were being restrained. "Why won't you let us go?" "Are you keeping us captive?"

I couldn't understand all of the different languages as they screamed. But out of the shouts I recognized one voice speaking English; he was a detainee from Chicago. In a short exchange with him, I remember that he couldn't understand why we wouldn't let them go. There was no explanation that I could have given him at the time that would have made sense to him or any of the prisoners. They couldn't understand that they were free, but in order to protect them - to help them - it was necessary to wait a little longer. They had no place to go, there were too many of them to release on the land, and the population was already overtaxed for food and the necessities of life. If they could have only understood.

The question of nationality didn't come to my mind. I don't remember seeing the distinguishing Star of David which has been mentioned by the press and others as being so prominent. However, the thin, tattered clothes they wore couldn't have supported any type of a decal. I have come to understand that the vast majority of the inmates were Russian and Polish which confirms my memory of the voices and languages. My first action was to give them the two or three K-Rations that were in my pocket. Later, as I passed that point coming back, I saw one of the inmates vomit. The food was just too rich for him. Another inmate ran to him and picked up his vomit, but I do not remember his having eaten it.

I wandered through camp until I found Downard standing with Captain Lummus at the rail siding. It remains a vivid memory - a mental picture at even the mention of the word Dachau. There were a number of boxcars, flat cars, and coal cars on the rails - probably about fifty. In each one of them there were bodies stacked up as high as five to ten feet deep, all being virtual skeletons with blank, hollow eyes. Even though I had been released from the hospital, my strength had not returned to normal and my resistance gave way and I vomited. More to the point, I vomited on Downard's boots. He was both kindly and sympathetic about the messy incident, nevertheless he masterfully moved to my side in case I should have to vomit again.

After briefing him on our defensive situation, he advised me that we were to move shortly on to the south and east with Munich as our target. Other details of our conversations escape me; it was hard to focus on his words as I stood looking at the atrocities surrounding me.

Some short time later after I had left him, I was told that one of the soldiers next to Downard shouted, "Colonel, here's a live one!" after having seen a hand move among the stack of bodies. Downard and a tank destroyer captain climbed over dead bodies to reach him. He was quickly transferred to the medical area that had already been established by the AMG. The DP had more clothes on and seemed in a better physical condition which was what probably saved him. Photographers from both Life magazine and the 42nd Division were there to capture the moment that Downard pulled him out of the stacks of bodies. I was told the photo made the headlines back in the United States. Later, a story circulated that the DP number 64923, a Pole named Gleb Rahr had survived and was to become famous as the sole survivor of the death trains. A miracle. (Editor's note: there has been additional, yet inconclusive information that another gentleman may be the survivor in Jack's account.)

On my way back through the compound to assume the duties that Downard had given to me, I knew full well that this was a historic moment. I took advantage of my time to see what I could. One tragic scene I won't forget was of an inmate crying and holding onto a lamp whose shade was made out of human skin, the tattoos being prominent in its decoration. I observed the stacks of bodies at various points and I knew when I got to the crematorium what had to have been taking place. The ovens were cold. I do remember that. I didn't witness the notorious "shower rooms" though. I passed the electrified fences, the guard towers, the moats, and the pens where the guard dogs were kept. Mainly I saw the administrative offices, the crematorium, the rail sidings, the service area, and the detainee compound area. Standing out in my memory was the extent and massiveness of the camp facility. I know now that most of its massiveness was in the form of service facilities. Adjacent to the section of the prisoners' barracks was the luxurious quarters of the SS Camp which acted as the commandant's headquarters. From the balcony of a beautiful three story building, an SS commander could see almost all of the squalid barracks of the prisoners and bark his orders to the guards. This section of the compound contained splendid living quarters, well-appointed gardens, and even a bakery on site just for the use of the SS. Such a vile contrast!

As I returned to my jeep, the sights and smells I had witnessed continued to sink in on me of the enormity, the beastliness, and the tragedy of what had happened here. It was man's inhumanity to man. This was one of the most distressing and depressing moments I've ever had. The haunting look on their faces will remain with those of us who witnessed Dachau throughout our lifetime.

Even though I had seen so much during the war to harden my senses, I now think that if we had known about the inhumanity the Germans inflicted on the people at Dachau, we would have had even more a sense of purpose in the war than we had developed early on. As I look back at the details and all the horrors of that day, the heaviness of those memories seems as if I was at the camp for days, when actually I was there for only about three hours before I was called to my next assignment.

A few days after the liberation of Dachau, I heard that the AMG had gathered officials from the town of Dachau and marched them through the camp areas and among the prisoners – forcing them to view the horrors of what had existed and what they had turned a blind eye to. They all abhorred what they saw, denying they knew what existed in the camp so close to their town. Most of them wore cloths around their faces to filter out the foul smells and possibly to disguise their face which might have been recognized by the inmates. As expected, they all cried out, "We no Nazis! We no Nazis!" For months to come, German civilians were forced to view the horrors. The inmates were detained for months at the camp under considerably more humane conditions until order could be established to return them to their homes, if their homes still existed.

CONTRADICTIONS

There are several contradictory stories regarding the opening of the concentration camp at Dachau. The combination of these stories tell quite a bit about the times, the operations of the American Army, and the effect that event had on our human nature. One of the stories which circulated regarded the 42nd and the 45th Divisions, and which division was the first to enter Dachau. As I know, the reconnaissance unit of the 42nd reached the eastern end of the concentration camp on April 29, 1945. They requested instructions to enter the camp immediately; however, because the advance troops were only about a platoon in strength (about thirty) in number, they were ordered to stay on hold and wait for the main body of troops.

A rumor was started that the "on hold" was made at Corps or Army level so that the 45th could enter the camp first because of its seniority as a combat unit. The 42nd wasn't about to let that happen, so a platoon of 2nd Battalion entered the camp for a few minutes, only to be ordered back outside the compound when the news of their entry got to an upper level of command. It wasn't until around 3:00 pm that day when an advanced party of 42nd officers and men entered the compound, supposedly in complete coordination with the 45th.

With this aside, the 45th Division vaguely mentioned in their history books that there were "other troops" in the compound at the time. By the same token, the 42nd Division makes minimal mention of the 45th Division's presence in its account of the liberation of Dachau. And, in fact, I didn't see any 45th Division troops while in the compound. That doesn't mean they weren't there. The compound was vast and there was chaos everywhere you looked. Additionally, the units were not wearing their identifying patches at the time, so you wouldn't have known one division from the other.

Around 3:00 pm on April 29th, Brigadier General Linden, Assistant Division Commander of the 42nd, went inside accepting responsibility for the camp along with Red Cross officials and news reporters. The "Stars and Stripes" reporters were there, and also, by some magic, in all the confusion there was a small bit of "pomp and circumstance". This seemed such a sad and revolting way of revealing these horrors.

A second rumor, which was a part of the liberation of Dachau, was regarding a "kafuffle" between officers of both the 42nd and the 45th. At this time, Brigadier General Linden, while inside the compound, went looking to contact a ranking officer of the 45th Division. He came in contact with a Major Sparks who challenged Linden's entering the compound in the area which the 45th Division had under control. In a rather heated discussion wherein Sparks was insubordinate to the point of insulting and cursing at Linden, it was stated that Linden struck Sparks with his riding crop. I had come to know Linden, and I believe his own account of the events which he addressed to the 42nd troops. He stated that in their physical posturing of each other, the General, not about to back down from a major, stood his ground waving his crop as he was gesturing to Sparks about his defiance. It was at that time that the Major inadvertently moved closer and into the General's riding crop. The 45th Division wrote a book on the incident much to the detriment of the 42nd. There were charges and counter-charges of cursing each other, the two striking each other, Sparks waving a pistol at Linden and other actions which made it difficult to believe any of the accounts as being accurate. General Linden was a gentleman, highly disciplined, and if only because of his training would never have stooped to such tactics with an officer of low rank as described by the source from the 45th.

If any part of the story was true, it was unfortunate, and unsoldierly, that a general and a major would let themselves get into such a situation. And, it would seem that Major Sparks should have been subject to a court-martial for rank insubordination to a general and assault with a deadly weapon on a general. They both went to court as a means of appeal for settling any misunderstanding between them. At the time of the situation, the events were quieted as quickly as possible because of the furious activity taking place in the compound at the time. Charges were later brought against Sparks, but were squelched by higher authorities.

Subsequently, the 45th brought the incident out again, and both the 42nd and the 45th, having excellent public relations and press corps, turned the incident into a doozy of a situation. In fact, I estimated that the most posturing was done by the public relations of both units. A tragedy. Nevertheless, the story grew and grew, each time distorted further to no credit for either the 42nd or the 45th. On the whole, it makes little or no difference which division entered first and time makes it even more trivial. The fact is that on that day, some thirty thousand souls were given some hope that their long and bitter ordeal was coming to an end.

PART IV: THE END OF THE WAR

CHAPTER FOURTEEN

ON TO MUNICH
APRIL 30, 1945

After the liberation of Dachau, the war went on and so did our march to Munich. On April 30, 1945 we headed to the suburbs of Munich having heard that there was a strong possibility Panzer units were going to take action against the Americans. A high-ranking German officer had taken command of troops in the Munich area and organized resistance in the path of the 42nd Division. As for the 222nd, any of the pockets of resistance we came upon quickly gave themselves up. Sadly, many of the German officers had erroneously been told that the Americans were not taking any prisoners and many of them executed their own men. They would rather see them dead than surrender.

The SS were the strongest factor in Germany's resistance; although they did very little fighting themselves, the cowards put forth their weary men to face the final blows from the Allies. There was evidence that pointed out that they used delay tactics to allow themselves time to retreat into planned caves, fortresses, or other places of protection (redoubt areas) outside of their main defensive lines in the Tyrolian Alps – all in an effort to reorganize themselves while their men fought on. Here in quiet caves in the mountains, the Germans stashed stores of arms, equipment and supplies – waiting for the moment they would be needed.

On our march to Munich, the landscape slowly changed, showing the great German war machine was coming to a close. Evidence everywhere pointed that they were out of fuel. Tanks, vehicles, generators, and tractors were abandoned along the road - even German fighter planes had been parked in their airfields. A German field marshal, after having run out of gas, walked a good distance to our company to give himself up. Even so, we could hear the distant rumble of artillery and incoming rounds to keep us all uneasy.

The Rainbow Division was ordered to attack elements of the German Army that were defending Munich and to secure the city. In the process, we saw the white flags of surrender on almost every home, factory and public building. Their show of surrender didn't prevent snipers and organized German units from using the flags as cover to continue their fight. Most of the German soldiers were hard to recognize because they changed into civilian clothes and had thrown their rifles away before they were captured.

One business stood out defiantly – Munich's City Hall. On a tall pole, right outside the entrance, was a Nazi flag flying high, an aggravating sight to all of us. As soon as we could move in on the huge building, the first thought in my mind was to tear down the flag. I lifted myself onto the roof and climbed up to the pole hoisting the flag. Instead of tearing it off, I managed to pull it off and stash it in the back of my jeep. The next day I was able to give it to my commanding officer.

As we searched through the City Hall, we found Germans dressed as civilians hiding in the offices. It was a chaotic day and many soldiers were wounded. The rotunda of the City Hall was crowded and filled with large wicker baskets full of confiscated metals – several baskets had pistols, others had eye glasses, dentures, wedding rings and jewelry, watches, knives, rifles, cameras, field glasses, etc. As we took over the building, the city servants lined up in the halls with white arm bands – and again we heard them shout, "I no Nazi"!

As we continued clearing our designated area in the city, an interesting incident occurred that I can't forget. As we approached a small cluster of buildings, a small bald man came running out waving a white flag followed by a large busty woman, probably his wife, beating him about the head and shoulders giving him a loud tongue-lashing. The man indicated with his arms and a few English words that there were soldiers in the building who were armed with machine guns and wanted to surrender. Through an interpreter, I told him to go back in and tell them to come out with their hands up. He did as I requested with the big woman still racing after him beating him on the head and calling him a traitor. Soon after, we were pinned down by machine gun fire. We aimed our bazooka and fired directly into the building killing all seven of the soldiers including the old man. It was somewhat of a mystery because we never found the big woman. After the blast, several soldiers in the surrounding buildings came out with white flags choosing not to fight further.

We finished our time in Munich and I waited in a convoy to move on to our next location as Lieutenant Davis, you may remember him from the vertigo incident, was in the process of clearing out some office buildings and banks. He had a fondness for using the explosives that our Mine Platoon possessed and couldn't resist the temptation. Startled by a loud "who-sh-omb"! I immediately exclaimed: "What has Davis done now?" Quickly I followed the sound and saw the front end of a bank building tumbling down with a cloud of dust as German marks blew into the air and began floating back and forth to the ground. Davis had over-charged the vault door literally emptying the bank of its contents, including furniture, fixtures – everything. Every civilian within earshot came running into the streets and gathered up all of the worthless money they wanted. What a sight watching them scurrying the streets for the floating bills, catching them in the air and fighting for each piece as it blew down the street!

CHAPTER FIFTEEN

ON THROUGH EUROPE
MAY, 1945

Next we marched to the town of Buch, where a similar incidence such as what happened at Munich occurred. After cautiously entering a part of the town, we again located the City Hall. Rounds of sniper fire started to come from the second floor of the building. After some time, the firing was silenced, but we didn't know if the sniper was dead, had left, or had taken another position within the building.

While waiting out the situation, an old man, who later proved to be the Burgermeister (Mayor), came from the back of the building towards the 2nd Platoon Troops bearing a white flag, only to be stopped by an older woman coming from the front entryway. She began reprimanding him and ordering him to go back into the City Hall. He walked past her and approached us explaining that he wanted to give himself up. He yelled that there were SS in the building who were dangerous and were under the control of his wife. In the meantime, she had run back into the building for a period of time, only to return saying that "her soldiers" had left, and continued the scolding of her husband. We cautiously entered the building and performed a thorough search. She proved to be correct; we didn't find any SS. When we left, we could still hear the Burgermeister and his wife arguing.

On that same day, a supporting tank destroyer had a track blown off by a land mine. As a result, the A/Ters were assigned to clear mines from major routes to the east of Buch. It was a time consuming field duty which didn't turn up further mines. But, during our search, we came into contact with a small German unit which, after the exchange of a few rifle shots, gave themselves up.

The German major, after seeing we were not going to execute his troops, confided in us that their equipment and supplies, which they had abandoned, had been booby trapped. Geary ordered the major and his soldiers to lead him to the sight of the abandoned equipment and then ordered the major and his soldiers to move the equipment and supplies - just to make sure the booby traps had all been removed. The German officer further revealed that an SS officer had been assigned to his unit to make sure they stayed in the field and fought. To the great relief of the major, the SS officer had disappeared and we were able to march the officer and his troops to a POW concentration point with only one of my men guarding them.

POWS

While we were clearing villages and collecting POWs, we still had to be on alert for surprise attacks. Only occasionally did we receive incoming artillery, but we were able to quickly silence their arms. One evening proved to be different when we heard the distinctive sound of a Tiger tank moving forward towards the unit. As we hunkered down ready for a battle, frightened for what we felt would surely be a deadly assault, the entire Tiger tank unit silently exited the tank and surrendered without a shot. We breathed a collective sigh of both surprise and relief.

Too many of the men from the Rainbow Division were now occupied inspecting, interrogating, and disarming Germans and we were left short-handed. As infantry troops in the front line of attack, we didn't have time to take the surrendering Germans into custody, nor were we prepared for handling the masses of them. At this point, we merely confiscated their arms, optics, knives, ammunition, grenades – any instrument which could be used against us, and instructed them to march westward as a group, until the Military Police could take them into custody. We had already reduced our ranks by sending soldiers back to guard prisoners, so we were hesitant about dedicating more troops for that purpose.

In one group of Germans marching toward us to surrender, their leader was a Lieutenant Colonel. He refused to surrender to anyone but an American officer. Men from my platoon called me over to help with the situation which led to his "officially" surrendering to me. He handed me a long-barrel luger pistol in a leather scabbard, explaining in perfect English, that it was a family heirloom that had been with him through the Russian invasion and had served him well. He asked me to take care of it with the possibility I would be able to return it to him one day. Along with the pistol, he gave me a pair of field glasses, a leather map case, and a leather back-pack, asking that I keep them as well. He wrote down his name and address on a scrap of paper I had in my pocket. I was suspicious of how he came into possession of the field glasses; they were of a make and style used in our Army and in excellent condition. I was also cautious about the luger and the other items - concerned that they may be booby trapped. But, for some reason, the bearing and conduct of this officer impressed me. The last time I saw him, he smartly saluted me as he marched his men in perfect formation down the road. I'm sorry that after all these years, I lost his name and address and wasn't able to return the heirlooms to him.

Rumors started spreading to the front lines that the war on the Western front was coming to an end – we had defeated the Germans! As excited as the men were to hear the good news, we still had our orders to advance and clear out the countryside of any remaining German troops, so there was little time to celebrate. We heard from patrols that there were still German units ahead of us who were capable of attacking and cutting us off, so we stayed focused and ready. At the same time, our prisoners had become an almost impossible problem. As we maintained our guard we still had to march hundreds of them, with their arms behind their back, to the nearest POW centers located throughout the country. The centers were already overloaded and didn't have the facilities nor the capability of caring for the enormous number of them. There was a constant stream of prisoners as trucks were shuttling my platoon back and forth from POW centers back to the field.

There were times when handling the POWs became dangerous. They would organize and attack the guards that were transporting them, or attempt to escape by hiding in the crowd of prisoners. At times, we knew of some of the more hard-core prisoners had escaped, but there wasn't enough guards to spare to leave the line to search for them. Our interrogations turned up several high-ranking officers dressed as enlisted men in the ranks, including SS. If the SS surrendered, they continuously caused further trouble by challenging the American troops and causing uprisings in the POW concentration centers.

COMMANDEERING A REAL BED

The German resistance that existed was in the form of night pillaging, sanding gas tanks, sabotaging equipment, slashing tires, etc. It was presumed that civilians had been organized to carry out these types of operations in the event the Americans came through their towns. They were creative and strung piano wires between trees across roads anticipating a jeep coming by and the wire cutting the soldiers' necks, possibly even decapitating them. There was so much of this type of activity that Army vehicles were soon equipped with wire cutters (aka "Stingers") mounted at the front of their vehicles. No retaliation was carried out, although the GIs using their initiative hinted to civilians that if it didn't come to a stop, many of them would be shot - starting with the Burgermeister.

Patrols were sent out in different directions to clear out the countryside of Germans and German resistance. Luckily Germany didn't use any of their stored munitions, explosives, nor equipment in our final sweep. Had they done so, there is little doubt we would have suffered a high number of casualties. Patrols discovered huge unused gasoline caches that would have been invaluable to the Germans. Why these caches weren't used when they were so desperate remains a mystery.

It should be pointed out that during this time in particular, and as unflattering as it sounds, GIs were not willing to be deprived of any conveniences when they could easily commandeer whatever they needed. At stops along the way when they knew that they would be in one place for a while, the GIs would commandeer a home, and at times, would run the owner and his family out. More often than not we would take over the home and have the family care for our needs.

For us to sleep in real beds was a luxury we had only dreamed about, so we took the opportunity when we could. Next of importance came a warm bath. In this situation the women of the family would wash our clothes and iron them – what a wonderful feeling to be clothed in fresh underwear, pressed woolen shirt and trouser. And clean socks! If there was food and drink in the house, that was a plus, but to sleep in a bed was a high priority even if there wasn't time to remove our clothes. We discovered that the Germans had a corner market on the world in beds and bed coverings with their down coverlets encased in fresh, clean linens. The women were for the most part immaculate housekeepers taking special pride in their cleanliness and airing of bed clothes. Too many nights we rested with probably less concern for our personal security and safety than we should have. A soldier waking up in a clean bed after having bedded down in dirty or muddy clothes and boots couldn't help but feel sorry for the frau who wrung her hands and cried on seeing her bed dirtied so badly. Almost always the men would try to appease her by giving her a chocolate bar or a cigarette.

On May 5th, the A/T Company was ordered to move eastward to the small farming community of Freutsmoos. It was a small dorf, possibly numbering eight hundred people. With the Anti-Tankers commandeering quarters for its one hundred fifty soldiers, the population was considerably burdened to provide beds for that many. In almost every instance a family was allowed to stay on in a part of the home commandeered as long as they were sociable. In certain instances, when we had suspicions about the family and their ties to the Nazi party, they had to be evicted to ensure the security of the soldiers occupying their home. While staying in the homes under these conditions did not create any particular good will, the civilians tolerated the situation, many capitalizing on it when their hospitality encouraged the men to share their coffee, chocolate, cigarettes, flour, etc. with the owners. As we would gather around the table to eat, we would discretely watch a member of the family take a bite of the food before we would join in, just to safeguard against poisoning. Recognizing the reality of their status, and accepting it with a degree of grace always led to a warmer relationship between the civilians and the Anti-Tankers. Time tendered this relationship to the point of friendship, especially later on in the occupation period.

While stationed in Freutsmoos, news came down from regiment that hostilities would soon cease. Although war was still going on in Japan, at least the war in Europe would be over. At the same time, headquarters suggested that the Rainbow Division was going to be assigned to the occupation of Austria after the cessation of hostilities. The stepped-up plan gave us little time to consider any kind of celebration. All of us found it hard to accept that the end of the war was near. As happy as we were, we could never let our guard down. We were still handling too many POWs and our headaches with them were compounded by thousands of civilians on the road returning home - most loaded down with belongings on every sort of cart, bike, or animal imaginable. It was tragic to see the older people having to suffer the extremes of relocation under the most difficult of circumstances.

CHAPTER SIXTEEN

VE DAY
FREUTSMOOS TO BERCHTESGADEN
MAY 8, 1945

May 8th, 1945 was VE Day – the war in Europe was over! Rather than get drunk or do anything crazy to celebrate, there was a noticeable calm amongst the troops, recognizing the fight was over. During these first few days there came a marked difference in the temperament of the Anti-Tankers. We became less stressed, more relaxed, and had a higher degree of self-confidence. For now, there would be no more killing, destruction of property, mistreatment of civilians, nor living and acting like beasts.

In the middle of our quiet jubilation, there remained a problem. Peacetime operations in a foreign and conquered land was something that hadn't been addressed in our training. How were the soldiers to deal with the vanquished? Who was to define how much the Germans were to suffer for their sins? Now that the war was over, was discipline to be relaxed? Was the soldier to do as he saw fit? Should he vent his anger on the populace? What now?

Fortunately, just as the military government had planned ahead for all the intricacies of war, they had also planned for peacetime. An extensive outline of the actions and conduct were already designed and ready to put into place. We were now in the time of occupation, and our duties were to remove any remaining threats to peace, help the decimated populace to heal its wounds, rebuild the destruction which the war had heaped upon them, and re-establish their economy to a healthy level.

Orders were made crystal clear that the GI's discipline would be held to the highest degree, security would be maintained on a combat level, and cleanup of redoubt areas was our prime objective. We were also to support and coordinate the military government with the newly established civilian governmental units. And, leaving little room for doubt, fraternization with the civilians was strictly forbidden.

COMMANDERS' ROAD TRIP

At peace, what a wonderful word! Before the time for occupation was established, Captain George B. Waters, now our commander, in his wisdom and knowing the needs of his men, immediately arranged for us to take some time off. The first group which was given consideration for leave included Second Lieutenant Bolt, First Lieutenant Harold B. McEndarfer, and myself along with several company officers and NCOs. On May 9th, we loaded into two jeeps and ventured into the Bavarian Alps. Excited to take a trip, our first destination was to view the Eagle's Nest, Hitler's infamous mountain hideaway located near the town of Berchtesgaden, Germany. To get there was no easy task and proved to be more time consuming than we had thought. We drove through the countryside and the valleys of Obersalzberg mountain, across the foothills of the Alps, and, finally, made the climb by jeep up the Kehlstein Mountain to the notorious site. Prior to reaching the summit, we passed some of the SS barracks, which at one time had housed security troops. Further on, we saw the villa belonging to the leader of the Nazi Party, Hermann Goering; it had been leveled with only the wreckage of his swimming pool identifiable. Once we reached the peak of the Kehlstein, instead of the glamorous and elaborate Alpine villa we expected, we found that the surface of the mountain top retreat had been leveled by Allied bombers.

The Eagle's Nest was a 50th birthday present from Martin Bormann; it was a residence Hitler hated. He had an innate fear of heights and disliked the thin mountain air and its bad weather. The construction of the compound ended only a few months prior to the end of the war, so he seldom visited it. When we arrived, we weren't even sure what we were looking at with only rubble left of the surface area after the bombing of the Allied planes. There was a small entrance that led to a tunnel which went down into the massive bomb-proof underground. Here, we stood in total amazement. We stood looking at a home which appeared the size of a small city and luxurious in every detail. Standing out in my memory is Hitler's dining room and its elaborate furnishings. Probably two hundred guests could be accommodated comfortably here. The dishes on the tables were gold with engravings that highlighted his "H" in the center. And in the library, thousands upon thousands of books, films, and reference materials lined the walls. Every room was decorated with furniture of the finest of mahogany.

The AMG were already present and in the process of establishing order by allowing visitors to come in and view some of the rooms while making certain parts off limits. I had the opportunity to get a volume of books and a reel of film from Hitler's library, as well as one of the gold service settings for eight. Later I painstakingly encased these pieces in plaster of Paris to ship home, but unfortunately they were confiscated by the Military Mail Service.

After seeing the Eagle's Nest, instead of returning straight to the base, we made a detour and drove up to the town of Gmund am Tegernsee, which is on the Tegernsee Lake, a seemingly bottomless glacier lake in the Alps that we had heard of. While viewing the area on a rented boat, we came upon an incredulous sight. With the most beautiful shores imaginable and completely surrounded by woods, we saw what was known to be one of Adolph Hitler's baby factories. The structure was a beautiful multi-story building, light and airy, strategically placed along the waters of the lake. As we steered the boat in for a better view, we saw motorboats, swimming paraphernalia, bathing suits, and all sorts of sports gear lined up on the deck near its entry.

It was well-known in the military that Hitler had designed and developed a program where he experimented in creating a superior race made of racially pure, smart, and beautiful Germans. The program, called Lebensborn, was ordered by Hitler and had the support of the German government. It was rumored that SS agents were sent out to kidnap babies and young children from qualifying parents, and were also instructed to rape beautiful women to produce perfect babies. The mothers were then brought to one of Hitler's sites, such as this one, and were well taken care of as they raised and educated their children in the institution...molding them into the perfect Nazi.

After seeing the unusual and haunting sights of both the Eagle's Nest and now the structure for Hitler's diabolical program, we came upon a local Catholic Church, went inside to sit, and take a moment to give thanks for the end of the war and the end of the cruelty Hitler had left behind.

We arrived back at our base camp in Freutsmoos, Germany, rested and ready to accept our next duty. Our first orders were for guard duty which included policing an area of one hundred square miles. It was a time consuming and highly organized search for any arms, knives, or anything considered a weapon within the civilian population. As we confiscated truckloads of contraband we recognized how the citizens were fully prepared and equipped to carry on the war on a local level. With this revelation, we stepped up our patrolling searches and seizures. Was the war over? Had peace really been established? No, not fully.

German soldiers started to emerge from their hideouts and give themselves and their equipment up as they began to realize that the Americans would not execute them when they surrendered. Interestingly enough, it became evident almost immediately that the German population didn't have a respect for the leniency with which the Americans were treating them. The people had been so strongly disciplined by the Nazi regime that they could only respect dictatorial authority. They thought of us as weak and wouldn't believe that we wanted to restore full democracy to them. Further, their attitude went from passive surrender to hatred for the Allies. We easily handled their lack of respect and it was dealt with firmly – maybe not as justly as we intended, but effectively nonetheless. We governed the local areas and if there were any breaches of the peace, the unit dealt with it.

One incident during this early stage of the peace which I remember was not a proud moment for me. An SS officer was discovered living as a civilian while carrying on some form of military activity. We brought him in to our headquarters for interrogation. One must understand that SS soldiers were highly disciplined, possibly the finest soldiers ever. This one SS officer was particularly adamant and belligerent. He continuously insulted and hurled abuse at the Americans who interrogated him. In trying to learn of his activities and any organization he might belong to in the resistance, we learned that he understood English quite well, although he refused to admit or speak it. After several hours of verbal interrogation and listening to his vicious insults, we made the decision to not send him back to regiment until we learned more from him. Physical abuse was used, mounting to torture to a degree. This form of interrogation was not allowed and wasn't acceptable, but nonetheless, it was used as a last resort in order to find out pertinent information. The SS man didn't break, and the use of our physical abuse was to no avail. None of us felt comfortable in what we had done during the interrogation and hoped we would never be put in that situation again.

PART V: OCCUPATION

CHAPTER SEVENTEEN

OCCUPATION BY THE UNITED STATES FORCES IN AUSTRIA
MAY 18, 1945

Soon after VE Day, the Rainbow Division became the military arm of USFA (United States Forces in Austria) under the command of General Harry Collins, 42nd Division Commander. Our division moved into Austria to relieve elements of the 36th and 45th Divisions who were to begin concentrated training for the Pacific Theater of Operations.

My division, the 42nd, was to control the American sector of occupation on the west side of the Danube. The eastern sector of Austria, on the east side of the Danube, went to the Russians to control. The southern sector was left to the British, with the French having little more than a presence there. The Anti-Tank company was to be located in the vicinity of Schwendt, a small dorf of about five hundred people located some fifteen miles north of Kitzbühel in a narrow valley.

The narrow valley lay between mountains which rose sharply to Alpine heights on both sides. Needless to say, most of the houses were built on the side of the mountains, a picturesque setting, but it made for a difficult situation in our hunt for housing. Although beautiful, the area was dangerous because it was recognized as a territory where the Third Reich had retired. Scouting, patrolling, or policing the area with any degree of efficiency was impossible in the mountainous area, so our efforts were mostly confined to patrolling on the road by jeep. Occasionally, patrols were sent into the mountains with little or no results other than showing our presence to the civilians in the area. On a few of our scouting expeditions we found evidence that connected the locals to a Wehrmacht hold-out in the mountains. We were disturbed to see the close relationship the locals kept with our nemesis and once we recognized this, we felt an intense distrust of the local officials and kept ourselves guarded and armed at all times.

Even in peacetime Davis was up to his old antics. This time it involved his access to explosives used by the Mine Platoon. One evening well after dark, while most of the officers were at the Company CP, our quiet evening was interrupted by a resounding explosion that was amplified by the walls of the valley. Our immediate reaction was to think this was terrorist activity. The company was alerted and a prepared plan was placed into action within minutes. Shortly Davis, having been noticeably absent during the excitement, came ambling into the orderly room with a devilish grin on his face only to discover the excitement. He quickly admitted to having blown up the bridge - the only bridge in Schwendt - and he had done a thorough job. It was completely destroyed! We couldn't get a satisfactory explanation from him other than he loved explosives and the bridge was there waiting to be blown up!

The civilians were frustrated, as one might imagine, and couldn't believe what had just happened. All available GIs gathered and hastily built a temporary crossing and soon after rebuilt the bridge with every intention of hiding the incident from Headquarters. If Headquarters had known about it, Davis' actions would certainly have called for his court-martial, something everyone – especially Davis – wanted to avoid. After the seriousness of the incident had somewhat subsided and the bridge had been rebuilt, we couldn't help but laugh at the whole event, particularly when we recalled the innocent expression on Davis' face. Even he would laugh about it, but only after several months when he felt comfortable that the matter hadn't reached Regimental Headquarters.

With so much energy pent up in the men, we had to release it in all sorts of horseplay, making for a lighter time; but instances like this caused our poor Captain Waters to gray prematurely. We respected him for helping Davis out, even when he didn't deserve it, and it was clear Waters had our backs.

RELAXATION AND PATROL

Toward the end of May, we moved to Thiersee, a village of about four hundred people located on the shores of Thiersee Lake, one of several lakes created when glaciers gouged out bottomless craters to be filled with water. The lake varied up to five miles in width and was some sixty miles long. It was breath taking with the clearest, crystal blue water you could ever imagine. The homes here were alpine in design sitting against the snow covered Alps. The weather was ideal; it was warm in the sunshine and cool in the shade. During time off, GIs would bask in the sun and enjoy fishing, boating, and hiking through the countryside. One too many times we tried fishing with a grenade or two until we blew a row boat out of the lake on one of our attempts. Yet, in spite of our antics, the people of Thiersee looked the other way and took our presence in stride, even laughing at some of our craziness.

The civilians we met were good, solid human beings. And after being cautiously coaxed, they were friendly with little resentment of our commandeering their homes for our quarters. More and more they were encouraged to occupy a part of their home and maintain it as we lived and ran our daily activities from it. The wall created by the war was slowly being torn down as the GIs and the locals came to know and understand each other.

We continued patrolling the larger areas mostly by jeep and truck. The size of these areas were far too great for any foot patrols, but we would periodically hike into the mountains to investigate reports of

German holdouts. There were many threatening situations, but we were able to resolve them by convincing the German soldiers that the war was over and they would not be executed. They would eventually surrender and their equipment was taken along with their supplies. In some instances, the equipment had to be packed out of the mountains by mule, but the ammunition had to be destroyed. It wasn't unusual to hear distant but deafening roars of munitions being detonated up in the mountains while the civilians carried on with their lives as if it was normal.

One day a worn-out Wehrmacht Colonel appeared at the 2nd Platoon Headquarters. He came down from his mountain hideout to negotiate the surrender of his major general. Although he did his best to bargain for terms in which the general would lay down his arms, they were completely unacceptable – we only allowed unconditional surrender. A five-man patrol made two separate trips up into an Alpine meadow, high above the timberline, to convince the general that we would not kill him and that he would be treated according to the provisions of the Geneva Convention. After hours and hours of discourse, he and his one hundred twenty five men finally marched down the mountain in an orderly manner with the 2nd Platoon patrol leading them into custody. Later we found this dangerously comical when the patrol realized how much equipment (enough to fight a small war) the German soldiers had at their hideout. We were commended but were cautioned to never take such chances again. But we did, time and time again with excellent results… and a bit of luck!

CHUCK BOXES AND BASEBALL

Rumors had floated throughout our division that there was a possibility we would be sent to the Pacific to aid with the fight against the Japanese. In preparation, we scheduled light training but it was done half-heartedly. The war in Japan seemed so far in the future that we couldn't wrap our heads around the thought that we would move on to another country and fight another war. Complex plans and schedules for training were drawn up to satisfy the higher ups that should we be transferred, we would be ready for our new role in Japan. The truth was that we were just performing to keep them off our backs.

From time to time, inspectors would show up to gauge our training sessions and to keep us on our toes. On one such occasion, we were using live grenades and ammunition during our exercises and a piece of shrapnel from a grenade hit the helmet of the inspecting officer. First startled, then angry, the officer gave us new restrictions on the use of live ammunition. On the upside, it lessened the intensity of inspections and the length of time we had to spend on Pacific training.

Patrol and guard duties occupied most of our time with considerable leniency for the weary GIs. R&R (Rest and Recreation) leaves were provided on a rotational basis. Some of the leaves were trips to Paris, London, the Riviera, and other dream-like vacations for most of us.

With some of the officers and men leaving for home, others on R&R, and the influx of new faces coming into the fray, military discipline became a problem. Two of my men "borrowed" an organ from one of the churches, loaded it onto a truck, and while one of the soldiers drove, the other played the organ while going up and down the street! As much fun as they seemed to have and as much as the civilians enjoyed following the truck singing and dancing, it was clear that it was time to do something to curb the leniency. The immediate solution was to keep the GIs constantly working and at times, entertained in organized activities. It worked. GIs were gathered in teams to play football or baseball in barren fields. With days getting warmer, we'd be in our shorts playing in empty fields with improvised bases and goals. Those days it kept many a GI from getting themselves in trouble.

As officers, our relationship had been regimented as we dealt with the seriousness of combat, but now, during peacetime, we began a new relationship. We liked to gather in the evening to visit, and, like any get-together - we loved to snack on food. We organized a "chuck box" where we shared all the packages that came from home. I was tempted to hide my package when I received a devil's food cake, but reluctantly I handed it over to the group. There was always a wide variety of packages that included: clams, kippers, tamales, chili, and all kinds of cheeses - all the way to turnip greens (I never had to share these!). It never failed to surprise me the variety of food choices that came from officers living in different parts of the country. Those were the best of days as we became close friends.

Again, we began to collect things which would make life more comfortable. For example, Davis found an abandoned trailer which had been used as a German field officer's office and quarters and Davis decided to make it his own. With a little redecoration and a few added comforts, he lived like a king. When we traveled in convoy, we began to look a lot like the French Legion when he appeared in line with his decorated and souped-up trailer. Admittedly, Davis had to move it discretely after it began to get noticed, but still, he kept it for some time as his personal quarters. As for the rest of us, we were able to acquire radios, bedding, favorite chairs, lamps, pictures, and the like, making our individual quarters more homelike.

The term "mess hall" was discarded as our cooks, Corporal Phillip J. Polski, Staff Sergeant Arnold C. F. Kubalsky and Technician Fifth Grade Salvatore M. Devine provided us as near a home-kitchen atmosphere as they could while we were on the move. At one point, the men of the company became somewhat disgruntled over the food we were being served. They all thought, and rightfully so, that there were too many dried vegetables. Being the platoon leader, it was my duty to solve the problem. One day, Kubalsky, who was one of the company cooks, and I took off in the jeep for a daylight reconnaissance and found a large potato field. It was illegal to barter with the Austrians so the only logical way to solve the problem was to have a "moonlight requisition" for the potatoes. We were reluctant to trust any of the men with such a delicate job that required an experienced hand to complete the mission undetected, so just the two of us took off that night for our new assignment. I clearly remember the two of us crawling on our bellies through the field digging and collecting potatoes as we went.

As we became braver, we began to hunt for rutabagas, dandelion greens, carrots, apples, or anything fresh. We became thieves in the night – something I'm not proud of but at the time I felt cleverly resourceful. There was considerable risk involved in doing this since food was scarce and civilians guarded their crops – as they should have. After a time, we decided it was better to barter, even though it was illegal. Frankly, we thought that we would prefer to be caught bartering rather than stealing – and it was certainly easier on our backs and our consciences. After we found our new path to requisition fresh produce, we found out that GIs were experts at bartering when it came to food; and this was their chance to shine! Fresh milk, beer, schnapps, German pastries, and all sorts of treats would magically appear on the dining room table with no questions asked.

I suppose this is why I never became a smoker. Cigarettes were in high demand on the black market and I couldn't see burning up the valuable commodity - especially at the exorbitant cost of $200 a carton. It was the most valuable of all of our tools to barter with. Each week we were rationed two cartons of cigarettes so I had plenty of available "currency". For what amounted to a very few cigarettes, a tailor would make me beautiful uniforms and I could buy hand-tooled shoes. I was able to replace all the clothing I had lost while in the hospital and buy gifts to send home without using a cent of my GI allowance.

To add to our collection of fresh food, we were lucky enough to come upon a unique opportunity while on patrol in the mountains. It had been rumored that in a remote area of the Alps, there was a doctor running a medical center; and so I took a couple of my men into the mountain to investigate his activities. After an exhausting search, we found him. I expected to see a full-fledged hospital, but I was mistaken. Instead, we arrived at a single-room clinic with an outlying home that belonged to the doctor. As he showed us around, we were further impressed by his credentials and the medical equipment he maintained. He was gracious in explaining the many advantages of the place, explaining that in case of an emergency, the clinic was the only source of medical aid that the people in the area could depend on.

He then took us to his home, a very small dwelling nearby, and introduced us to his daughter, who was home on an extended leave from Harvard. She had been in the US all during the war and had just obtained a visa to come visit her dad. I must tell you that I was immediately taken by the young woman, even though I couldn't follow how she had managed the visa since it was so soon after the war.

The doctor spoke perfect English and was starved for American conversation. He invited us to come back again when we had time to fish and he would show us a trout stream. The very next morning we retraced our steps to the aid-station. Right off, we were terribly disappointed to find that his daughter had departed to a village below. We felt sure the doctor considered that it would be better for her to be out of sight of a bunch of GIs, and we couldn't blame him. We did, however, go on to catch some one hundred fifty Rainbow and Brown trout. It seemed that as soon as we put our line in the water we would catch a fish - the stream was literally boiling with big, beautiful trout. That night we took our catch back down the mountain to our cooks and fed two hundred and ten men with the fresh fish.

THE SHEEPHERDER AND THE SS

We received orders dictating that we were to enlarge the territory in Austria that the Americans occupied and policed, so the A/T headquarters was relocated to Kreuth, Germany - another charming Alpine village. Here again, the setting was splendid, similar to that in the movie, "The Sound of Music". The territory was in the mountains and demanded all our resources to search and police the endless mountains. The physical requirements of hiking up the steep mountain slopes, then crossing a valley and going further upward on a higher slope were exhausting because we had to lug heavy equipment and weapons with us. The days were warm for hiking but the nights in the high country were mercilessly cold in our light sleeping blankets. We didn't sleep much, but dozed off and on as we tried to keep warm by a fire. We had heard plenty of stories about the German holdouts in this redoubt area and we knew we were easy targets day or night, so we had to keep guards posted outside of the fires where we slept.

One late afternoon while I was stationed at our command post, an elderly sheepherder of eighty two years, dressed in Alpine motif, and the customary "lederhosen" (leather shorts with suspenders), came running in to see us. With the help of an interpreter, he explained that his home was in a meadow far back in the mountains and that his wife was being held hostage by about twenty five SS. He tearfully pleaded for soldiers to go back with him to rescue her.

The interpreter couldn't get a solid story from him and we became suspicious he was leading us into a trap. However, he was clearly very upset, so I took a couple of men and set out to follow him up the mountain to his home, carrying a mortar and shells in case of an ambush. At first we had little concern about keeping up with the old man, considering his age, but it didn't take long after leaving the floor of the valley that we realized he was in better shape for the ascent than we were. The barrel-chested man was used to the steep climb, and he had to continuously wait for us to breathlessly catch up. He finally offered to carry our 60mm mortar and shells to help speed up our pace and, still, he out-paced us as we panted our way up the trails. Darkness caught up to us and despite the pleas of the old man to continue, we had to stop for the night, refusing to go on in the dark through unfamiliar territory. Admittedly, we all felt a little relieved when we stopped for the night and could rest.

Early the next morning after a sleepless and fireless night, we followed the Alpiner up the mountain. His home was located in a meadow with a couple of outbuildings close by. Arriving at his home around 2 pm, we immediately dispersed in a line from the buildings. After a heated talk with him, I forced him to go into his home, tell the SS they were surrounded (but not to mention there were just three of us), and that they would not be executed but would be properly released. Reluctantly, he proceeded. After about an hour, he still had not returned. There was no sign of him. We decided to take action and fired both a mortar round and a bazooka rocket, toward the house to get his attention - narrowly missing the house and unintentionally blowing out the corner of an outbuilding. This brought rifle fire from another outbuilding located at the back of the house. Just as we were preparing to blast the outbuilding with a bazooka rocket, the old timer appeared on the porch of his home waving a flag and yelling for us to stop. He approached my vantage point, and told me that the SS had disappeared into a cave that was located one hundred yards in the back of his house.

Since he didn't tell us of the cave's existence early in our questioning, we became even more suspicious of him. We held him with us during another miserably cold night. We now looked at the situation as a larger and more dangerous one and tried in vain to reach the company command post by radio, in hopes of getting artillery or even an air strike to come to our aid. However, our location was too remote to get a signal. At dawn I decided to have one of my men approach the house under cover as Private First Class Archie R. Monaghan and I cautiously approached the house with the old man walking at our side. After deliberating and accepting his assurance that only his wife was in the house, we entered cautiously to find that he was indeed telling the truth. There wasn't anyone in the house but a very scared little old lady. Frightened and barely coherent, she was able to tell the interpreter that the SS had all gone into the cave the night before.

A search of the outbuilding from which the rifle fire had come found that she wasn't quite accurate. In the outbuilding we found two women dead, shot through the temples, and an SS major laying on a mattress, bleeding to death. The major had shot his wife and their eighteen year old daughter, then turned the pistol on himself only to find he was out of ammunition. He then proceeded to saw into one of his wrists with a dull knife and draped the hand over a washbasin – it was three-fourths filled with blood when we had arrived. He was more dead than alive. After having surveyed what had taken place, an angry Monaghan stuck his pistol in the major's mouth and blew the back of his head off - much to the disgust of the rest of us. Both the major and his wife were in their early forties, and their daughter had been a student at the University of Munich. She was beautiful in the paleness of her death. All three deaths that day were a tragedy of the war. It was just so useless. Their fate was a product of Germany's fierce dedication for a cause, even to the death of loved ones.

Pressing on to find the other SS, we crossed the meadow and approached the cave the Alpiner had told us about. We entered through a tunnel that led to the opening of a massive cavern. We entered with caution, calling out to the SS to surrender, but there was no sign of them. Instead we found a sizeable store of weapons, ammunition and food. Further back, we found hundreds, if not thousands of treasures in carefully-crated art: paintings, statuary, tapestries and the like. Some of the crates contained ingots of silver. Continuing the search of the cave and surrounding area, we never found the German SS.

Besides discovering the millions of dollars of art, we uncovered a cache of cheese and Norwegian sardines. The cheese was in toothpaste-like tubes and the tins of sardines were fairly small. We sat on the crates and right then and there, we ate all we could!

After our feast, we departed the cave and because it was almost nightfall, we spent the night in the old timer's home with him and his wife graciously feeding us food and beer. Even with his hospitality and gratefulness for our help, we maintained our suspicions and kept our guard all night. The next morning, we found our way down the mountain to the command post to report our findings. The following day, one of my men led a team from USFA up to the cache. The disposition of the materials, nor extent of its value was never revealed to us, but we knew it had to be large. With a guilty conscience I never reported Monaghan's dastardly deed. I realized that a good soldier had weakened under his grief for the major's family and he had finished what the major had wanted.

CHAPTER EIGHTEEN

OCCUPYING WESTERN AUSTRIA
JUNE, 1945

The war had been over for a month and the lives of the soldiers had already begun to take on a different meaning. The peace that was coming gave each of us a new outlook on life. It was changing us back toward the individuals we had once been. Our occupational duties and training came more into focus and replaced the stressful duties and dangers we had experienced during the war. Young men began to think more about their future. They could plan and it felt good to be alive! Now that the war was over, it didn't take long for the soldiers to take advantage of the unique opportunities of being in this foreign land, to learn about it, and to see all of it they could.

Even so, we kept in the back of our minds that there was an underlying threat that we would be sent to the Pacific and the invasion of Japan at any time. Our training periods for the new kind of warfare we would be faced with, was only for two or three hours daily. However, not all of us had to participate. Several of the officers were excused to resume duties associated with the occupation. Guard duties, patrol duties, company duties, and other special duties cropped up – all of these responsibilities had to be taken care of as a first order of importance. As the days went on, we felt more and more pressure to emphasize our training and yet our obligations to the occupation of Austria were expanded. It was a busy time.

HITTING THE BIG TIME

In June, the Anti-Tank Company was reassigned to an area which included a part of the state of Tyrol, Austria, just east of Innsbruck on the Inn River. The area was so mountainous and was so difficult to patrol that most of our efforts were limited, giving us more time for training and recreation. There still was the concern of German holdouts in the back areas of the Alps, however, the Army was taking a "wait and let them come out" stance. Ultimately, this position lessened the danger for soldiers since we didn't have to go into the mountains and ferret out the hostiles.

We were quartered in a monastery outside of Fiecht, which had previously been used by German troops, and fortunate for us, it had not been re-occupied by the Catholic Church. A large part of the monastery was a magnificent cathedral – as were all of the Catholic churches of the country. It had been beautifully maintained, was staffed, and served the A/T Company perfectly during our short stay there. The buildings within the compound of the monastery had three stories and were large enough to provide a private room for each us – an unbelievable extravagance. The rooms were small and cell-like with only a bed and a chair. Even with the sparse rooms, we were still happy they were private. This simple convenience made a marked difference in everyone's attitude.

One day, on what was looking like a quiet, peaceful, and beautiful Sunday afternoon, the serenity was broken by a call from Staff Sergeant William J. Kluck. Apparently, a disheveled farmer had gone to a checkpoint with a story of a farmhouse that was loaded with valuables. A recon party led by the executive officer from the A/T Company had verified the find. Davis, who was in the recon unit, again used his explosives to open up a brick wall that was hiding silver and gold. Our company was called upon to drive our trucks to pick up the bounty. Upon seeing Davis at the farmhouse, he greeted me with "Jackpot"!

There in the middle of all the rubble were coins totaling approximately $2,000,000! The bullion consisted of silver mark pieces which had been canceled by deformation. After a call to our command post, it took a total of fourteen half-ton trucks to carry the sacks of silver bullion to a designated USFA point. Needless to say, that took care of our quiet afternoon. A story appeared in the Stars and Stripes Army newsletter a few days later, but no mention was made of Davis. Once again, Waters pleaded with Davis to be a tad more discrete in the use of explosives in the future!

A QUIET CHANGE

As time passed, guard and patrol duties became more and more routine. We still apprehended German soldiers who were in underground holdouts, but most of them were hiding in homes and trying to blend in with the populace. There were still indications of groups of SS hiding in the remote mountains; their locations were noted but had not yet been investigated. It wasn't unusual for a civilian to come into the command post to negotiate the surrender of one or more German soldiers who had attempted to blend into the crowd.

Civilians seemed to be less worried now that they had come to realize that Americans were not as vindictive as they had expected of conquerors. Some civilians, who were suspected of extreme collaboration with the Nazis, had to be arrested if we found they had committed crimes against the public during the war. This one point gave the Austrians confidence the Americans wanted to restore peace without stripping the country.

Innsbruck, Brenner Pass, and the Tyrolian Alps provided ample opportunities for soldiers to explore the countryside in their time off. We were even provided transportation to do so. The scenery was unbelievably picturesque and the quaintness of the dorfs and towns was intriguing. Most all of the businesses began to reopen to meet the curiosity and zeal of the young GIs and their paychecks. The Army sponsored clubs in the dorfs for the GIs to go for their beer, schnapps, and some entertainment. Even though we were getting used to more freedom, it wasn't difficult to enforce a requirement that we go in pairs for safety when we left the compound. The locals accepted our presence, although they seemed to do so reluctantly. They too were having to adapt to a new environment.

After a couple of weeks, the A/T's area of occupation expanded again, this time taking us deep into the heart of the Tyrolian Alps to the town of Wörgl, located in a narrow valley on both sides of the Inn River with towering mountains rising steeply from the valley floor. Troops again relied on commandeering quarters from civilians and sharing the homes with the owner as best they could. USFA was worried about the security of the GI, but as we developed better relations with the community, there was seldom a problem. It was reassuring to see civilians respond to the warm and friendly overtures of the GIs. Likewise, they were more cooperative and made life easier with each passing day. They assumed the role of providing a home-like atmosphere for the GIs in return for a little chocolate, coffee, tobacco, etc. As the military and the civilians came to know each other, our likes and dislikes, we found we had a lot in common and started to appreciate one another.

Although we still kept up our patrols, restrictions seemed to relax more and more over time. This concerned the USFA that our cleanup of holdouts would not be as thorough, but we still managed to uncover caches of munitions, looted art treasures, military equipment, food, and every supply you could think of. Every bit of the loot was turned in to USFA collection points where they gave out the clothing and food to the GIs, but the munitions and weapons were destroyed. Although the overall scene in the communities seemed peaceful on the outside, evidence continued to expose more problems that we would have to contend with at some point.

With more time in the compound, there was more time to prepare for a possible transfer to the Pacific. We studied the tactics for the Pacific area as well as field and night issues that could come up.

Plenty of rumors began to crop up about the 42nd being split into task forces to be shipped out earlier than had been expected.

In May, after Germany's surrender, the war department designed a point system called the Advanced Service Rating Score, with the idea of applying a sense of fairness to the release of service men. Each GI was given points for the months he was in the service, each star or commendation he had been awarded, and to those added the number of dependents the soldier had waiting at home. Once the soldier had collected eighty five points, he was eligible to return to the US. With the threat of being sent to the Pacific, more and more soldiers were applying for their points so they could ship home. Going away parties became an almost weekly occurrence and their replacements were sent in. We saw the solid camaraderie that the A/T Company had developed over the months slowly disintegrate as we spread out and saw our friends ship home.

RAINBOW UNIVERSITY

After a few weeks in Wörgl, A/T's occupational duties were changed once again and we were sent to Morzg, a suburb of Salzburg. All of Austria was breathtaking, but Morzg was special. It lay in a majestic setting with the towering Alps bordering its valley. At certain times of the year, the Hohensalzburg Castle, one of the largest medieval fortresses in Europe located on top of a hill overlooking Salzburg, would cast a shadow over the entire dorf. A/T, along with the 1st Battalion of the 222nd, were put in a Task Force to be on standby just in case there was any sizeable action which might occur in the western half of the USFA American Sector.

Among the most important undertakings for Major General Harry Collins was the establishment of the Rainbow University within the 42nd Division. Aimed to educate our own American soldiers, Collins gave me the honor of teaching a few classes for those GIs that wanted to further their education. I taught two classes in Trigonometry and later an Engineering Drawing course. Additionally, someone in high command decided it would be a good idea to organize a boxing program for the division. True to form, I committed to the endeavor. With both of these jobs adding to my responsibilities, I lacked the time to oversee my platoon activities, so for a period of time, I relinquished my responsibilities to Geary.

Classes for Trigonometry and Engineer Drawing were held in the barracks, but the boxing camp was a different matter entirely. I first set out to create a training camp for the boxers outside of Salzburg. It was fully equipped for feeding, housing, and training the division boxers. Miraculously, I was able to find Al Fontana, a professional trainer and previous athletic club owner and operator who ended up in the Rainbow Division. Al took care of the training and I organized, equipped, and operated the camp. Fontana's expertise made it a showplace, providing the division with championship boxers for Intra-Division and Supreme Headquarters Allied Expeditionary Forces (SHAEF) competition. The camp operated during our entire occupation of Austria but after a period of three months, it was consolidated with other training facilities and I was allowed to get back to my platoon duties.

SALZBURG FESTSPIELE

My time wasn't limited to just spending hours at the boxing camp and teaching courses. As it came to happen, GIs received an enormous cultural gift that summer. Morzg was located a small distance from Salzburg, the home of the famous Salzburg Festspiele. The annual music and drama festival had begun in 1920 and now, for the first time in eight years, Salzburg was able to have its beloved festival – three weeks of music in which leading musicians and composers would meet to honor their predecessors and to display their own talents. It seemed as though all of my fellow officers felt as I did, and wanted to fill every moment with the culture of the area. We would dress in our finest uniforms, neatly cleaned and pressed and our garrison side hats slightly tilted on our heads, to attend the concerts held in a special musical hall, an old and historical building. Most of the time, the performances were standing room only – and usually those were all GIs.

Prior to the war when we lived normal lives, we would have never had the opportunity to sit and listen to Schubert, Haydn, or Johann Strauss, nor learn to appreciate the atmosphere of string music. As I sat quietly, shrouded with the lovely music, I wrote notes in the program as to which composer I liked best, which of the frauleins sang with the most fervor, and which concert was my favorite. On one choice in the program I wrote, "I have a weakness for beautiful string music. In the orchestra, they have thirty five violins, seven cellos, seven basses, and a beautiful harp. How far I have come from the front line to find myself surrounded by such beauty."

VJ DAY

A monumental day came on August 13, 1945 - the end of the war with Japan. The announcement sent feelings of relief throughout the world, signaling that final moment of complete peace from war for the first time in many years. To the soldiers in Europe, it meant that our nightmare of shipping off to Japan was not going to happen after all. Many GIs felt that they had been given a reprieve - a chance to finish our duties in Europe and then be able to go home. They would not have to experience the horror of war all over again. Not unlike VE Day, it was indeed a day to be celebrated. But in Europe, instead of noisy and boisterous celebrations, there were quiet, thoughtful and prayerful periods. It really was over.

When we realized our fears were over, we all felt a wave of homesickness. We discussed it with each other, admitted it, and sympathized with each other. And, because it all took place with good friends, it was all okay and we could go on from there. But the day would always hold a special place in our hearts along with May 8th, both were days on which we would always be able to cry and say a silent prayer.

BAD GASTEIN

As a boy I had read in the National Geographic and Good Housekeeping magazines about a place called Bad Gastein and a spa hotel that was located there. It stuck in my memory because my mother dreamed out loud to me of wanting to go there one day. I clearly remember that in the early 30's, the cost of staying in the exclusive health spa was over $200 per day, an astronomical figure in those days. And now, with time and my money saved, I was given the opportunity to visit the spa and ski town on an R&R leave. My jeep driver, Monaghan, drove me through the Alps to the "Shangri-La" of my dreams – Bad Gastein!

The town of Bad Gastein lay in a high valley of the Hohe Tauern mountain range on both sides of a river with a rushing waterfall in the center of the town. Even in early September, snow covered much of the little Alpine village and ice ran down the stream. Because it was located in a gorge, the jeep was barely capable of making the last few miles of steep, winding mountain roads up to the timberline. Approaching my Hotel Europa was nothing like I had experienced before. Its magnificence could be felt even on the drive entering into the reception port for guests. I was treated like I was one of the royalty who had frequented it; I had never experienced such service. After checking in (there was no registration, you only gave them your name) I was guided to my room with my luggage to come later. My room was large, well-lit, and appointed in exquisite taste. I remember the carpets, their pile so deep that "I had to part it with my hands to pass through"!

That night I was taken to supper by an attendant. He first asked me if I would prefer to eat alone or in the company of another guest. I chose the company of another guest. The dinner and conversation was lovely, like nothing I had ever experienced before, including French dishes and pastries, wine, coffee – the works. The week I was to spend there was to enjoy such luxurious living as one can only dream about.

Each day centered on the daily mineral baths and massages. The bath house was immaculate in white tile and stainless steel fixtures with a recess in the floor. Within the recess was a seat, which once I sat down, hot mineral water slowly filled the tub to just under my chin; I was allowed only ten minutes to languish in the smothering warmth. Afterwards I understood why they would only let a guest stay for a limited amount of time, because after begging to stay a little longer, I had to be pulled out by two attendants! I was in such a weakened state after being in the mineral water my feet wouldn't hold me. A professional massage followed each bath lasting twenty minutes. Afterward, the masseuse gave me a bath – appropriate in that I neither had the strength nor the ability to stay awake long enough. After the first bath, I was wheeled while still on the massage table to my room where I went to bed and slept twelve straight hours. Each of the baths I experienced resulted in my sleeping from eight to ten hours.

When I wasn't sleeping, I took long walks along the quaint streets and dreamed of what would have been there in time of peace. The art galleries were especially intriguing – with prices far out of the reach of a young lieutenant from Rule, Texas. I also went to the inactive ski area where I got my first taste of a sport of which I had only dreamed. I rode a lift to the top of the mountain system and admired the beauty of the tiny village that straddled the silver ribbon of a stream far below. This was my Shangri-La. Paradise. After this taste of honey, it would be difficult for me to deal with mortal fellows again.

COMPASSIONATE LEAVE

After my R&R, I returned to Morzg, and within only a few days I received a call from my brother, John, who was located with his unit in Livorno, Italy. He was a technician with a heavy armor maintenance unit that supported the Fifth Army in North Africa, Sicily, and all through Italy. They had some of the worst assignments of the war with long days, nights, weeks, and months of nonstop repairing and maintaining of our war machines. In the call, I learned that he was to ship out within the next three days to go home for discharge. He had been overseas longer than I had been in the service and it would be a year or so before I would be eligible for rotation back to the States. Since it would be two years before I would see him, I was able to get a "compassionate leave" of seven days plus travel time to Italy and back.

My driver, Private First Class John J. Nonamaker and I left immediately with my jeep loaded with gasoline, K-Rations, cigarettes, wine, and other items which could be used as trading (bribing) material on the trip through the French Zone and Northern Italy. The two of us drove all day and night, and arrived at Livorno.

As I scoured the endless rows of warehouses and scanned hundreds of GIs roaming about doing their jobs, I saw a figure that I would have known anywhere. To start off, I yelled – "Jiggs!" – the nickname I had given my brother when we were kids. He stopped, stared at me, grinned, and then immediately put his finger up to his lips so I would be quiet. But it was too late. The fellows in his outfit only knew him as John and they now started heckling and kidding him with his new nickname. This marked the first time we had gotten together as men and the first time in years that I felt a sense of family. As boys we had, like most brothers, been adversaries to say the least. Now it was different. For now, we both treasured the opportunity to be together and we intended to make the most of it. Within a few hours of our meeting, an announcement came that his shipment was delayed one week. What luck! We now had the chance to take a few days together to explore Italy. We hurriedly grabbed supplies and took off on a road trip. Our plan was to first visit Pisa, then venture on to Florence, Rome, and Naples.

In Pisa, we visited the Leaning Tower and other sights with which Jiggs was already familiar. In Florence, he was able to show us a number of art galleries. And in Rome, we visited with a friend of Jiggs, a professor at the university, who arranged a visit to St. Peters

Cathedral and to Vatican City - both unforgettable. While we were there we were able to call home. Imagine a couple of west Texas boys calling home from Rome! But when we went to Naples, we were disappointed. The city was demolished, the harbor was filthy, and we didn't have time to visit the more beautiful parts of the city. When our time had ended and we returned to Livorno, the two of us said our farewell, promising each other to continue the closeness that we had found.

After our tearful goodbye, Nonamaker and I began our long trek back to the company which, in the meantime, had been transferred to Vienna. The route that took us to Vienna was entirely different from the one that we took from Salzburg. We went through central Italy to Padua and on to Venice. Our leave was extended two days so we could take advantage of the opportunity to see Venice. We stayed with a British unit that was quartered in one of the nicer hotels while occupying the city. The glass blowers and artists enthralled us as we walked through the streets and visited St. Mark's Cathedral, took a tour of the Doge's Palace and floated the canals on gondolas.

I recall that at dinner the first evening, the main course consisted of one small boiled potato, six beans, a sardine, half a beer and a cup of tea. Dessert consisted of a cookie. On seeing this, I got up, went to the jeep and came back with some C-Rations that we hadn't used. The British officers, equally hungry for food were overjoyed with the treasure and took us to be their new best friends.

From Venice, we headed northeast through the heart of the sparsely inhabited Alps. The trip was a long winding highway that followed small streams in the bottom of the narrow valley. At every turn we were in awe of the beautiful scenery. Upon leaving the Alps we saw the peacefulness in the plains along the Danube and around Vienna. The trip was one of the best times of my life, and yet we looked forward to getting back to our company and our friends.

CHAPTER NINETEEN

VIENNA, AUSTRIA
SEPTEMBER, 1945

Upon my return, I learned that the 222nd had been appointed as an Honor Guard Unit by General Mark W. Clark, Commander in Chief of US Forces of Occupation in Austria, with its headquarters in Vienna. We found the city to be in deplorable shape from the bombings and strafings that had taken place during wartime. The city was divided into the American, British, French, Russian, and the International Zones. These zones were open for traveling except for the Russian and International Zones which were "off limits". Their zones were guarded tightly and were highly secretive as were all Russian activities during the occupation. There were plenty of stories which circulated of soldiers who had gone into either of the two zones and disappeared under mysterious circumstances.

After having been selected, the 222nd was sent to Vienna to do our duties within the area of our zone. First on the agenda was to send out an advanced party to secure our quarters in the XVIII District of Vienna. Again, the practice was to select homes and buildings according to the company's needs, acceptability, and strategic locations, and then commandeer them. The advance team would knock on the door and give the inhabitants thirty minutes to gather up their things and vacate. However harsh this sounds, you have to remember that the Austrians were still our enemy. They were mistrusted, and the American soldiers' safety came first. There was a more formal "requisition of quarters and facilities" that took place afterward but it was only a formality in the commandeering process. Since all the officers were visibly armed while confiscating the premises, there was seldom a problem with the inhabitants leaving the premises.

We were lucky to have been assigned to the XVIII District of Vienna, one of the nicest of the suburbs of Vienna with beautiful homes and gardens which had been spared from so much of the destruction of war. For the officers of the Anti-Tank Company, the home selected was a luxurious chateau at 26 Buchleitengasse, which backed up to the Vienna Woods (the park of which so much has been written in verse and music). The chateau belonged to the Sass family - a prominent, wealthy, and dignified family. Papa Sass was a cabinet maker by profession, but early on he had accidentally stumbled onto the invention of the original zipper back in the 1920's. Still holding onto the patents, he was enjoying the wealth from the royalties. Herr and Frau Sass (Papa and Mama, as we came to know them) were in their late seventies. They had their daughter, grandson and granddaughter living with them while the daughter's husband was in the German Army.

When we went to commandeer the home, we had a problem. The Sasses had not been notified by government officials that we would be taking over their home. Seeing how we came to their home without their having any prior knowledge, our orders were met with indignity and outrage:

"We will not leave!"

"We are not animals to be turned out of our own home!"

"What are the Americans? Heathens?"

After they saw their approach wasn't working, they changed their tactics. More effectively, the Sass family began pleading for us to not turn out old and sickly people – expounding at length on the sad plight of their situation. In the end, Mama and Papa Sass broke down and started crying and sobbing. This was too much for the American officers! So, as a compromise, we agreed that the Sasses could keep the servant's quarters and be put in charge of keeping the house clean for the officers. With no interpreter, all of our negotiations were in the Sass's German and the American's English ... plus a lot of sign language. Neither party knew the other's language but we managed to come to some sort of an agreement – what that agreement was, neither of us were for sure. Frankly, we were relieved to be away from Mama Sass's heart-wrenching sobs.

The Sass chateau was probably the loveliest in modern Vienna. It was a two-story home with eight bedrooms - each with its own bath - marble floors and a large living room, study, library, sun room, and garden room. It had a huge dining room that was probably 30ft x 50ft that could easily seat thirty people comfortably, a beautiful kitchen in white tile and stainless steel, a breakfast room, sewing room, workshop, a detached servants' quarter for two, and a four-car garage. The gardens surrounding the chateau were large, manicured and breathtakingly beautiful – all with the backdrop of the Viennese Woods.

After we settled in to the home and began our daily routines, it wasn't long before Mama Sass began to interject herself into our lives, insisting that Papa Sass help her look after "her boys". Whatever suspicions we may have had with her pampering and attentiveness, they were soon overcome when the genuineness of her concern became more apparent. She was a true lady and Papa was a gentleman from the old world and they knew how to handle us with finesse and charm.

Shortly, we were drawing our rations from the mess hall and giving them to Mama Sass and her daughter. The women would take our meager provisions and make delicious meals for all of us. As we were to learn, even the wealthiest and most powerful citizens of Vienna were struggling and hungry and they were grateful we shared any food we could requisition. In return, the quarters and our clothes were kept immaculate. It didn't take long for Mama Sass to exert her own authority on us. She never wavered when she needed to fuss at us for coming in too late, or God forbid if we had a little too much to drink or if we partied excessively; her discipline was needed and accepted.

We knew that Herr Sass had been a Nazi, although the extent of his involvement couldn't be determined. We assumed that he was avid and many times we brought the discussion up to him, but we never heard or sensed an acknowledgment involving Nazi activities. We expected that, and would let the subject go. While we were staying there, the Sass daughter heard of the death of her husband on the battlefield. We were sad for her loss, however we couldn't sympathize with any sincerity. This certainly didn't help the situation. Afterwards, we recognized the possibility of her becoming vindictive. Although she never showed any, it was still hard to have a good night's sleep. We slept with a pistol under our pillow and many times one of us would stay awake and "on guard" while the rest slept.

In Vienna, as in much of Europe, the people loved their music – so much so, that they made listening or playing music a tradition in their families' daily lives. This held true for the Sass family. Tuesday night at their home was chamber music night. On that first evening, we found it to be a command performance (Mama's command!) and no one was allowed to miss their tradition. But after the first time we complied with her wishes, we never needed any further encouragement. We put on our best suit for the occasion and were on our best behavior. After dinner, we would gather in the study where the performance took place. Mama Sass played the baby grand piano, while Papa Sass played the violin, their daughter played the viola, the granddaughter played the flute, and the grandson played the clarinet – all classical instruments. For the most part, the officers didn't understand nor appreciate the classics, but Papa Sass, using his grandson, Frankie, (who spoke English) as an interpreter, gave us brief lectures on the classics. The evenings were lovely and very formal. Papa and Frankie dressed in white ties and tails while the ladies wore long dresses.

When they took a brief intermission, Mama Sass served us glasses of their local wine.

Those nights were some of our best memories of Vienna.

In one of the Sass's garages was a Mercedes Benz limousine, sadly it was jacked up and without tires. It had a chauffeur's compartment with seats for eight in the back – all with comfortable leather and beautiful wood trim. Along with my colleagues, we managed to take our company jeep wheels off, metalize and rethread them, put them on the limo, tune up the twelve cylinder engine and set it on the road. Most mornings, Bolt would put on a driver's hat and play the chauffeur while Papa Sass sat in the rear seat, with his hands on his cane and his head held high as they drove through the city. What a sight! Papa Sass made sure the Mercedes limousine could be seen all over Vienna. The engine was never fully tuned, and was knocking on military gasoline, but it ran well enough for Papa Sass to feel on top of the world.

The XVIII District was adjacent to an old area of Vienna known as Grinzing. The name, "Vienna", is German for Wein or city of wine, and Grinzing was one of the foremost wine growing areas in the world. Each year in the fall, the city had a festival to show off their latest crop of wines. Under the wing of Papa Sass, we were given a grand tour of the Wine Festival where he introduced us to the festivities and tastes of all the local vineyards. The colorful native traditions, as so elegantly brought into focus by Papa Sass, were pure joy to participate in. The wine tasting inevitably got out of hand and Papa would have to help his boys home afterwards – or maybe it was his boys helping him home! Regardless, Mama Sass gave us all a sound lecture on our arrival home - no interpreter was needed to understand the fullness of her intent. The sincerity with which it was delivered couldn't be resented in the slightest – it was well deserved!

The particular locale of the Sass mansion was in a delightfully wooded and flowered part of the district. There was a little Catholic church nearby and small shops were gathered around a community hall. The "Hall" was nothing less than a beer hall where people gathered and had their community events including dances, parties and "beer-busts". We always enjoyed attending some of these lively events and participating to the degree we were allowed with any discreteness. The local people seemed to want to accept us but with the darkness of the war still hanging over their heads, it was difficult. And it showed both in their posture and their interactions. Nonetheless, the quaintness and niceness of the neighborhood added to the charm of that part of Vienna. The architecture of the buildings was in the style of the homes there, and the Austrians would never completely ignore the Alpine motifs that made them feel comfortable.

The Sasses, having seen the lack of culture in the young men, were determined to see that we took advantage of all the available activities in Vienna. The local opera house had been destroyed early in the war, but being lovers of the arts, the Viennese made it a priority to have their opera, ballet, and concerts restored as soon as possible. It happened soon enough, and fortunately for all of us, we took advantage of the unique performances. The Sasses organized the trips; all of us dressed formally. Papa Sass wore a top hat, white tie and tails, and Mama Sass wore formal evening gowns and a tiara (furs were outlawed then). We loaded into the limousine with Bolt chauffeuring and off we went to the opera on Wednesdays, a ballet on Thursday, and a symphony on Saturday.

All of the GIs were enamored with the operas and ballets. The operas never failed to put a tear in our eyes and we found the ballerinas beguiling as they gracefully leaped onto the stage. They would twirl and lunge, and raise their elegant arms into the air. However, as a side note, we couldn't get use to the sight of their thick, long, underarm hair. The dark clump seemed to ruin the mood. As much as we enjoyed their performance, I could never shake the image off! But just as much so, I will never forget the memory of Herr Sass following the score with an enjoyment that shone in the expressions on his face. It's a picture I'll never forget.

A neighbor couple who was a good friend of Papa Sass, Herr and Frau Tempe, came into the picture shortly after we arrived to Buchleitengasse. Herr Tempe, a highly intelligent man, was a retired Vice President of the Austrian National Bank. He immediately took a liking to each of us and was interested in our backgrounds and well-being. At seventy years of age, he was one of the most graceful skiers I've ever seen – soon converting us into skiing enthusiasts. Herr Tempe owned a magnificent hunting lodge up in the mountains outside the city, a short drive from their home. It was possible to ski from the lodge, using the fire-breaks in the forest, to the back gate of the Sass Estate – some twenty miles, all being downhill.

He trusted us with his hunting lodge to use at any time to ski or to hunt pheasant or Chamois, a small goat-like mountain antelope. We would hunt as we skied down, stopping mid way to make coffee on an open fire and enjoyed sandwiches Mama Sass had made us. There was never a problem getting one of the men from the company to drive us up to the lodge; they always enjoyed the Alpine drive and the luxury of the hunting lodge. Technician Fifth Grade Boda C. Heath, an Arkansas GI, was always available to drive us up, especially after his unfortunate ski accident where he "straddled a tree" – since that time, he preferred to drive! Spring skiing was so warm that we found ourselves substituting sweaters and wool pants for bathing suits. In July of that year, we even skied on a glacier near Salzburg in our bathing suits!

After reading of all the activities we enjoyed during our time in Vienna, the question comes up, just how did we have enough time to enjoy all of these activities? Due to the discriminatory "point" system which applied to the release or discharge of officers, the military kept an inordinate number of officers on duty in Austria. The normal compliment of the Anti-Tank unit was seven officers, but at one point there were eleven of us assigned to the company. By organizing our duties, it was possible for an officer to receive one twenty four hour tour of duty every tenth day so there was plenty of time for enjoying activities in and around Vienna. And we did!

CHAMPAGNE FOR EVERYONE

Although there were always random problems that came up from time to time, the basic duties during our time in Vienna were to provide guard duties at various points within the American Zone, provide a security force at USFA headquarters, and most importantly, to provide a presence in the Austrian capital. We were always making contact with the British, French and Russian garrisons to consult on activities within the zones, and when asked, our patrols were sent into the international district to help with more urgent or delicate events. One night a patrol of eight or ten of us went to the Danube River Port to inspect and take over a motor barge suspected of having illegal cargo on board. This was a joint operation with a Russian patrol, coordinated by an officer at regiment. After muddling through the challenge of gaining entry to the port, finally getting on board the huge motor barge, and putting up with a suspicious and overbearing Russian patrol, we found that the barge indeed had an illegal cargo of champagne – thousands of cases of the pink bubbly. After commandeering the cargo and waiting for orders on how to dispose of the cargo, the command came down to release the barge, its contents, and its crew. After seeing the Russians help themselves to several cases of champagne, we decided to help ourselves to a few cases as well. We took thirty cases - all that we could safely get on a one and a half ton truck. It's easy to imagine the celebration we had that evening when we drove to the company area with enough champagne for everyone!

VD AND THE GI

By now, many of the Anti-Tankers had been rotated home and were replaced by either new recruits or replacements from other divisions. The young, new recruits were fair game for the vices the big city had to offer, and many of them were intent on taking full advantage of it. Most were extremely young, away from home for the first time, and wanted to put in all the excitement that they could in the shortest time possible. It seemed that they were hell-bent on self-destruction. Fraternization with the young Austrian women was illegal and yet the enterprising GIs were able to find the young frauleins and party with them on a regular basis. In actuality, the no-fraternization rule was not strictly enforced. All of this led to a surge of venereal disease. The problem became so severe – with a 6%-10% increase per month - that it was necessary to have a VD (Venereal Disease) Officer to combat the infections. The responsibility fell on me.

My duties were enormous. I had to give regular lectures on the subject, provide instruction and materials on how to prevent the disease, plus I had to keep statistics of all the cases. Additionally, I was responsible for apprehending the offending GI and getting him treatment and also apprehend his source and see that she got treatment. The most immediate and common method to prevent a GI from getting a venereal disease was to enforce prophylaxis, or "pro", as the servicemen called it, which was an application of chemicals to the genital area – usually within two hours after having sex. If a group of guys were found in an area known for prostitution, they were forced on the spot to have the application, a very degrading circumstance to find yourself in. Fortunately, penicillin was available at the time and very effective, but it was only available through Army medical sources.

One of the sadder stories that I heard concerned a young GI, fresh from Stateside, who having heard the stories of the beautiful frauleins, free flowing booze, gambling, etc., entered into that aspect of his Austrian tour of duty with full exuberance. Unfortunately, he contracted syphilis within a few weeks of joining his company. With the knowledge that penicillin would cure the disease, the ordinary GI would take it in stride and get cured. But this young fellow was out of the ordinary. He was very conscientious in his personal habits, his self-pride, and his concern over what his parents might think about his actions. Having accepted treatment and counselling, the young GI still couldn't cope with his predicament and he choose to commit suicide – a tragic ending to a young vulnerable life.

A GRAND CHRISTMAS IN VIENNA

Time sped by and before we knew it, the snow was falling and the holidays were approaching. This was to be my second Christmas away from home and I was homesick. Christmas had always been a special time in my home, one of special family togetherness. For now, the Christmas of '45 was looming ahead, the war was over, and I could think of a million reasons why I didn't need to be in Austria. I should be at home. But it wasn't to be, so I forced myself to once again make the best of the situation. Christmas in Vienna!

During an evening meal one night, a group of us got the idea to put on a Christmas party for the children in the district. With plenty of enthusiasm, we began to explore ideas and as soon as we could, we got to work. Local wood shops were put to the task of making toys for the kids. We arranged a buffet by saving our rations as well as moonlighting a few additional items to provide goodies for the party. After a heartfelt request, talent from the local opera and ballet volunteered their services; and the opera house loaned us the costumes and setting to make sure it was a special presentation. Our efforts developed into a major happening. Soon, the plans leaked out and caused a lot of excitement in the community as well as in our own regiment as we prepared for the big day.

We chose the local beer hall for the festivities. Describing it as a beer hall does it an injustice because it was more of a community center where the men in the community gathered almost daily to tell their stories and, on occasion, women and children would join them. It was a large wooden structure that could seat six hundred people comfortably, had a stage, a bar, and it even had a dance floor. It provided everything we needed for our party and we intended to use every inch of it. It didn't take long before the plans became so massive that a major was put in charge to see that our plans were carried out to completion. It was going to be an extravaganza!

After weeks of preparation with cooks, carpenters, musicians, electricians, and lots of enthusiastic GIs, the big day came. The whole neighborhood, especially the children, were filled with excitement of an actual Christmas party, something that hadn't happened in years for them. At eleven in the morning the party began.

The children filed into the beer hall orderly with excellent behavior and beautiful, smiling faces on every last one of them. Of course they attended with their parents who, at first, were suspicious of our intent. Just how could these soldiers who had recently participated in a full blown war against them, be trusted with the well-being of their children? But they came in the hundreds and it was a joyful sight for all of us. These big, tough men suddenly remembered their instincts from when they were kids and gave themselves completely to the children. We had planned for each soldier to take three to five children under their wing during the party, but we had no idea the outcome would be so successful. Moreover, the Austrian adults relaxed when they saw how the children and GIs responded to each other.

First off, the children were served sandwiches, cookies, fresh fruit, and hot chocolate. We had saved the chocolate bars and instant milk from our K-rations for weeks to make them the delicious hot chocolate. The cookies and the sandwiches from potted meat came from the K-rations as well. The children took to it immediately, gobbling down the new delicious food and drink that they were so unaccustomed to. But, almost immediately after, the children became sick by the richness of the food and began violently vomiting on the tables, their chairs, the floors. A total smelly mess! The scene seemed disastrous, but the astute GIs scurried around cleaning up the tables and floors and calming the children as best as they could to save the moment. Some of the children's delight was dampened. Dampened, but not lost. To console them, we made a quick change so they could take the food home to enjoy a little more slowly under the guidance of their parents.

Next, with a little adjustment in schedule, the Vienna Ballet staged a Christmas presentation to the music of the Vienna Symphony. The children of Austria were brought up to appreciate the extraordinary music of the opera and ballet, so it was a happy time with the actors, dancers, jugglers, clowns, elves, animals, wooden soldiers and the like, in a maze of merriment on the stage, up in the balcony, and out in the audience. We were entranced by the children's reception and their enjoyment of the festivities. Even the children's upset tummies returned to normal.

But it wasn't over! Next, came the best part of our festivities. The children from Austria didn't know about Santa Claus but instead were visited by the "Good Angel". The idea of replacing Santa with a Good Angel took some adjusting to by most of the GIs. Many of them were insistent that it had to be Santa Claus who passed out the gifts, but the cunning (and beautiful) ladies of the ballet swayed their thinking.

Then the magic began. The beer hall went dark for a moment and a quiet awe crept through the room. Earlier a cable and harness arrangement had been invented by some of the fellows allowing the "angel" to descend from the ceiling to the floor of the hall. Answering the murmur of the kids, a brilliant spotlight shone up into the vaulted ceiling of the hall, highlighting a gorgeously costumed angel – complete with a flowing gown and dazzling white wings. With beautiful, classical Christmas music in the background, the heavenly figure floated slowly to the stage. One of the dancers from the ballet dramatically assumed the role of the "Good Angel", gracefully making her way through the room passing out gifts to each of the children. She was a lovely and kind-looking woman and gave out the gifts with a tenderness only an angel could have had. It was a sobering moment for all of us to watch the joy in each child's eyes. They were then given a wooden toy, some fruit and candy, and afterwards the party came to an end.

The entire ceremony lasted about four hours, but many of the parents and children stayed behind to visit and soon, we became fast friends. Some lucky guys were even invited by the parents to spend Christmas day in their homes. The camaraderie that developed between the Austrians and the GIs was an unexpected benefit.

Though we were giving the party, we ended up receiving the best gift of all. The Christmas Day festival we created was one of the most memorable Christmas celebrations we would ever know. Many of us learned for the first time the true meaning of Christmas – the love and sharing among our fellow man. It was good for a troubled people, and some very troubled soldiers, too.

CHAPTER TWENTY

ASSIGNMENT IN LINZ, AUSTRIA
JANUARY, 1946

An important part of the Army's strategy was to move troops around frequently. There are numerous reasons for this, including sharing the more rewarding duties such as the one we enjoyed in Vienna. All good things have to come to an end, and our plush assignment had to be over as the 222nd might be getting a little too accustomed to the niceties of Vienna. And so, we were moved again.

In mid-January the A/T Company was transferred to Linz, a city in north central Austria, located on the Danube River. Across the Danube from Linz was the town of Urfahr. Linz was a light industry town which fortunately hadn't been bombed a great deal during the war and was already making a comeback. The Danube River was designated as the boundary between the American and Russian Occupation Zones with the Americans occupying Linz and the Russians occupying Urfahr. The difference between the Americans and Russians in their attitudes toward occupation and reconstruction - and their attitudes toward the civilians in general were as different as night and day. You could see the change happen at the very point the bridge crossed the Danube, dividing the zones.

Our first assignment placed us in quarters that had been an old school building. While quite a contrast from the homes we had been living in during our stay in Vienna, the rooms were nonetheless comfortable, warm, and adequate. Our duties were to provide motor patrols around the city and outlying countryside to monitor the activities of the civilian population. Even now, the civilians were still suspected of being potential troublemakers. There was a lot of abandoned German equipment laying around the area which only needed gasoline or a tweaking to put them back into operation. We recognized that almost anyone could have collected the firearms, ammunition, knives, photo equipment, radios, and other military paraphernalia from wartime and use it to strike back at the Allies. We immediately began our collection of the contraband. The civilians who held on to the gear were threatened with prison if they didn't cooperate and turn it in.

Shortly thereafter, the A/T Company was given the additional duty of guarding the bridge across the Danube. To be more convenient, our quarters were moved closer to the area where we worked. Once again we gathered our belongings and moved into what had previously been the German Marine Barracks. What a letdown! We shared tiny bedrooms that were depressing to look at and were old, smelly, and in a bad state of repair.

And just like our accommodations, our duty at the bridge was a drastic change from what we had done previously. It was a wide and modern highway that contained both a railroad and a pedestrian crossing that were always in use. We were to maintain eight to ten men and one officer on the bridge twenty four hours a day, seven days a week to control the civilian traffic and maintain security at the entrance. Although there were no attempts at that time to blow up the bridge, there were a number of legitimate alerts that kept us on our toes.

The principal behind controlling the civilian traffic was to keep even more people from becoming displaced persons. It seemed that the entire Eastern Europe population, controlled by the Russians, wanted to migrate to the west and into the American-British-French Zones. The civilians desperately wanted to get out of the tyranny of the Russians in their zone of occupation. Every day we heard stories of the cruelties the Russians inflicted against the people on the east side - apparently with no reason other than the Russians' nature for meanness. Most of the Russians had been in the war for years and had seen their homeland burned and destroyed by the Germans, their women raped, and their elders and children brutally killed. And now, they seemed intent on getting vengeance. The Russian soldiers' general mentality made the situation even worse. There was no question as to why the people wanted to get into Western Europe, just as there wasn't a question as to why we had to keep them from migrating. Western Europe had undergone enough destruction and deprivation without having literally millions of people come in to add to the problems of housing, food, clothing and the like.

Every day thousands of people came across the bridge for work or for legitimate business or personal reasons. Each person going into Linz, had a pass or papers which had to be inspected by the Russians and likewise, the Americans had to check on the paperwork of those going into Urfahr. The large majority of citizens had legitimate passes. Even so, their belongings had to be searched for contraband. If contraband such as guns, gold, silver, art, industrial parts and other illegal material and goods were found, they were confiscated and the offender had to be arrested. Those pedestrians who didn't have paperwork or a pass would beg and plead for us to be merciful and let them go across. To our chagrin, we had to turn them back.

During our assignment at the bridge, we experienced a variety of issues with the civilians and were forced to make hard decisions. Most of the difficulties came from older people who had suffered during the war and were now having to cope with the hardships they endured at the hands of the Russians. They wanted to cross the bridge to escape the intolerable conditions they were forced to live in. It was a terrible struggle for each of us to have to turn them back. I remember a couple of instances that stand out where, right or wrong, we interceded. One such instance was regarding a young and desperate woman who had no papers, and without any other means offered herself sexually to a

Russian officer in exchange for the right to cross. Of course the nasty human being took well advantage of her offer and before it was over she had been taken into a room, and she had been raped, not only by the officer, but was then passed around to several of the other Russian soldiers. Afterwards, she appeared to be bleeding badly and needed medical help, and so we gave in. In full few of the jeering Russians, we helped her into a jeep and transferred her to a nearby hospital. In another instance an old woman walked across the bridge and when she was approached by a Russian guard, pleaded with him to let her cross so she could die in her home in southern Germany. She offered a diamond earring to the Russian officer as a payment; he immediately jerked the diamond off her ear, taking part of the cartilage with it. But, before she could cross, other Russian soldiers who saw her bribe, decided to beat her for leaving them out of her negotiations. She was bruised and bleeding so heavily, I took her to the hospital where she was safe and able to get treatment. The next day her grateful cousin came to me with a tissue-wrapped gift – the other earring! The Russians had neglected to look for the other earring under her hair as they struck her.

CHECKMATE

In general, the officers and men of A/T, by nature, wanted to become friendly with the Russians. After all, we were Allies and had fought in the same war for the same victory. What more could we have had in common that would encourage us to be friends? In our best attempt, we invited a Russian soldier or two to eat with us at the mess hall. They came, but invariably they caused problems which made us regret the invitation we gave them. Their ill manners, uncouthness toward civilians along with their personal hygiene were so offensive, that we held our breath until they left. The Russian officers seemed more tolerable because they had fairly good manners and were somewhat more congenial, but we found even they were rude and foul mouthed about everything American – food, clothing, housing, games, social graces and the like.

It was difficult for us to communicate since we didn't speak each other's language. The only interpreters we had were the civilians from the bridge who at times would work in the mess hall. Still, we continued our visits by using the sparse Russian or English language with neither of us being very fluent. During one of our visits, the Russians wanted to play a game of chess with us. As it so happens, chess is the national pastime for Russians and they were champions at it. On the other hand, we knew very little of the game, if we knew it at all. The Russians, while offering very little instruction on the game, would "checkmate" us in no time, then burst into laughter and berate us for our stupidity. We took this good naturedly until the time came that we insisted on teaching the Russians one of our games - dominoes. Aha! The tables were turned and it became clear that the Russians were better winners than they were losers. Upon losing the game the Russian officers would curse at us, turn over the table and take the dominoes outside and throw them as far as they could. As time would tell, there were just too many differences between us to overcome. It was easy to see that the two nationalities were virtually incompatible and our attempts at dinner, games, and conversation had to come to an end.

THE SCHENDLERS

After months of duty in the occupation of Austria, I had yet to be able to secure a ticket home. Fortunately, I was able to get relief from time to time to explore and get to know the people of Austria. On one of my random excursions into the countryside I came upon an older farmer, Herr Schendler, who, with his family, struggled to make his crops and keep his farm working. After what seemed like a short visit, we took to one another and became fast friends. In what soon became routine, I would secure rations from the mess hall, take them to the family, and stay with them as much as a week at a time. I was always treated like family. In the mornings I put on my lederhosen and worked side-by-side with the farmer helping him milk his cows, hay his animals, cut and bind the grain, and all those things that are needed on a machine less Austrian farm. The returns of my endeavors were huge. Once again I had been fortunate enough to find a pseudo-family to fill my longing for home.

Frau Schendler was no different than Mama Sass and so many others. She could take my rations of sugar, flour, coffee, and chocolate along with the other ingredients I was able to snitch from the mess hall, and make wonderful meals. This was ample reward enough, but to have the opportunity to go fishing with a real "troutmeister", Herr Schendler, was icing on the cake. We spent a lot of time on the icy mountain streams pulling out Brown and Rainbow trout – and there was really no fishing to it. The fish literally jumped to us! We would just put our line with a fly on it in the water, and seconds later we had a pan-sized fish. We spent hours doing this, enjoying the beautiful surrounding country and all the while, Herr Schendler would explain and dramatize stories or points about the area. I returned the favor by telling him about my home and life in Texas. He was enchanted by my description of my home, the land, crops, livestock, and the people. However, he was a bit disillusioned that Texas didn't have the Wild West, nor the Cowboys and Indians they had always heard about.

Schendler was an educated man and spoke English well. He did his best to teach me the German language, in spite of my annihilating phrases with my Texas accent. For that reason, the Schendlers spoke only German to me in the household, except when explanations deteriorated beyond recovery. I learned later that the Frau and their son spoke English fairly well too, but they wouldn't practice their English on me because of being restrained by Herr Schendler, who was intent on my learning German.

On Sundays I frequently attended church services with the family. They were Catholic and very formal. With the help of Schendler, I had learned enough German by that time that I could follow the sermons with some success. The church itself was magnificent. Even in the smaller communities, the churches had ornate architecture, stained glass, and glossy pews. Only in going to mass with the family (they had a young son and a baby daughter) was there any degree of discomfort and feeling out of place. This put some pressure on the family but they never mentioned it unless I brought it up. It wasn't that I wasn't welcome, nor that I stood out in the congregation, but it was as if the people resented their respite from their suffering being intruded upon by a source of their suffering. You couldn't forget that most, if not all, of these families were missing loved ones because of the war. Was I the one that deprived them of their father or son? I understood their feelings and was relieved that there was never a confrontation nor an unpleasant instance resulting from my intruding in their lives. After church, we went to the local community center where locals held their parties, at which there was no shortage of beer and schnapps. The parties were pure pleasure as we put our troubles aside and enjoyed the fellowship, good music and dancing, the beer, and good food.

ILLEGAL CARGOS

Back on the base and back to our daily routine at the bridge, we became bored. Our boredom turned into creativity, and as such, we managed to get ourselves into trouble. While I had been in Italy, I became familiar with the owner of a Cognac distributor – Hennessey 5-Star Cognac – a choice liquor. After a quick call and a day or two leave, some of the fellows and I took a couple of two and a half ton trucks on a trip into Italy and brought the trucks back to the base loaded with cognac. We, in turn, sold them to the Russians for $50 per quart profit, making us quite rich in a matter of just a few days. Illegally rich! The irony of it all was that we were paid in "occupational script" which was virtually worthless as there was nothing to spend it on nor could it be converted to the American dollar. All this risk was in vain. But as the good American soldiers that we were, we supplied everyone in Linz with cognac and we soon became heroes! The Russians, too, were glad to get it, although it was illegal for them to get drunk. It seemed interesting that they could drink liquor, but that it was illegal for them to get drunk! Not that the law mattered much to them. On the bright side, we were never caught, and some of us enjoyed the wickedly dishonest feeling for having done such an illegal act.

In another attempt to make a little money, one of my colleagues used his wits to profit off the Russians. During the war, and even now during the occupation, the Russians were scourged with venereal disease. They had already heard that the Americans had penicillin with its miracle cure and they openly declared they would pay anything for the drug, no matter how they could come by it. This piqued the interest of one enterprising GI. He found that he could go to the hospital and gather up all the empty penicillin vials, fill them with a colored liquid and sell them for $1,200 per vial. The only trouble he had was in matching the color and consistency of the liquid to the penicillin. After a little trial and error, he found that urine was the perfect match! So the order of his day was to piss in all the empty vials and then make his sale. His business flourished without his ever being caught. Take that, Russia!

MASS MURDER OF RUSSIAN POWS

While in the Linz region, men across the division were tasked to train guard duty to escort various types of prisoners to other locations in Europe. They would be notified that they were to go on prisoner guard duty and told to pack a sleeping bag and appropriate rations for the amount of time they would be gone. Some of the prisoners, like the higher-ups in the SS, were taken into Germany for the war crimes trials occurring at the time. Others, like the Russian POWs, were taken from the relative protection of the POW camps into the Russian zone under the most unfortunate of circumstances.

As a consequence of the German aggression, many Russians had been taken prisoner. The Geneva Convention meant nothing to the Germans and they brutally mistreated their captives. As a result of the Germans' inhumane treatment, many of the Russians, acting to save their lives, renounced their citizenship of Mother Russia and took up arms for the Germans. In time, the number of Russians who became soldiers for the German Army amounted to entire regiments with most of these troops being utilized on the Western Front against the Americans, French, and British. Previously, Stalin, who ruled the Soviet Union, insisted these Russians should be returned to Russia's control at the end of the hostilities. Their allies, not varying from the rules of the Geneva Convention, carried out the agreement to the last letter ... the very last, bitter letter.

There were many events which made lasting impressions during the war and then afterwards, but for many, there were none that could have left a scar more than some of these Russian-prisoner turnovers. In particular, the British faced some very difficult moments which have been well documented. The prisoners knew their own people and the iron temperament with which they would be judged, and they were terrified to return to Russia and face their certain fate. To facilitate the turnover, the Russian prisoners were collected from their work camp and loaded into the forty and eight railcars for what they believed to be the prisoners' tortuous thirty six hour trip back to Russia.

The stories that have come out about these turnovers state that each railcar was divided into eight cells which were divided by wooden slats to separate their cargo. Each wooden slat was padded to protect the prisoners from using them to do bodily damage to themselves. The prisoners were stripped naked so they couldn't use their clothing to hang themselves and special care was taken to confiscate any instrument, no matter how small, so they couldn't use it to commit suicide. It was sub-zero weather outside and there were no stoves within the boxcars, not even straw on the floors. The ratio was one soldier to every two prisoners to prevent them from killing themselves, but even with this, there were a number of prisoners who succeeded in ending their life in the most inconceivable ways.

At their own request, prisoners would try to choke each other by reaching through the slatted walls to their neighboring cellmate. They would chew the veins in their thighs and ankles so as to go unnoticed as they bled to death. They would do anything to escape what they knew lay ahead of them. Somehow a knife, a nail, or some other ingenious instrument was secreted aboard the train and the prisoners would pass it through the slats from one to the other. Each taking turns in an effort to slit his wrist with the dull blade. It was a duty to keep them alive until the turnover took place, but the horrifying and cruel nature of the trip, and the pitiful cries of the prisoners constantly begging to be executed in their cells was almost too much to bear. It would have been a disturbing and shameful time for every soldier who had to fulfill this cruel assignment.

After the train reached its destination in the Russian sector, all of the guards, except for an officer and two soldiers, were replaced by Russian soldiers. The prisoners were then marched into the Russian Zone. As soon as the Russian Commandant accepted the prisoners, the train guards were ushered to a vehicle that was waiting for them in the Russian compound and escorted back to the zone they had come from. Within thirty minutes, firing squads barked out the non-judicial sentences. This happened time after time, train load after train load – each time the trip taking more of a toll on any soldier participating in train guard duty, and creating more disdain for the Russian allies. It would be difficult for those involved to shake the feeling that they were an accessory to mass murder.

CHAPTER TWENTY-ONE

DEACTIVATION OF THE RAINBOW DIVISION
APRIL, 1946

By the end of April 1946, the occupation of Austria had developed to such a point that an organized armed force of the size and capabilities of the 42nd were no longer needed and the higher powers were ready to deactivate our forces. The German Army in Austria had been demobilized, their manpower dispersed, and their equipment destroyed. The Allies had re-established local governments and had delivered a sound peace back into the communities.

As much work as we had done, there was still so much to do. It didn't seem to make any difference that the redoubt area of the Alps still had pockets of resistance, and there were outbreaks by SS and other die-hard German troops. Although many of these pockets were being removed along with their caches of equipment, we knew that there were more - possibly many more - of them which existed. Additionally, civilians still harbored resentment of the Allies and their terms of unconditional surrender. Everywhere there were reminders of the concentration camps and their internees, as our efforts to help the communities return their lives back to normal were far from complete. Still, provisions were made that on the departure of the 42nd Division, policing authority would be shared between Allied Command Forces for Austria and their local specially trained police forces.

We had a lot of apprehension in making such a move because it could potentially invite rioting among the hungry and downtrodden citizens. Turning over guard posts on the Danube River to the Russians understandably threatened the Austrians. It is interesting to note that the Americans had more concern about their ally – the Russians – than about their enemy, the Austrians. But that was the situation. In spite of our deactivation and being able to go home, many of us had genuine concerns for the people we had grown to like and respect.

From this point, and for some reason I don't understand, I was assigned to take over the German POW Camp in Hallien. Initially, I was to take over the kitchen facilities – feeding five hundred Germans two meals a day. But fortunately for me, for I thought it to be an easier assignment considering my skills, I ended up with the responsibility of the POWs, guarding them and taking responsibility for their well-being, including their medical care and any health problems they might have. We had the understanding that the POWs were less like prisoners and more like detainees who would be released at a future time to return home to Germany. Not knowing what I was faced with, I was more than eager to take on this new responsibility.

Slowly, I began receiving the Germans into a ready-made prison. First there were the initial two hundred, followed by the remaining three hundred. I had twenty five non-commissioned officers to help me with the organization. Because of the Germans' training and self-discipline, we had minimal difficulty with them. Most of these POWs had been fighting in North Africa and were between the ages of thirty to forty years of age. They had been through a difficult time in their duties in Africa and were intent now on becoming model prisoners and being able to go back to "Der Vaterland". They all wore boots, German-issued shorts, were bare chested and muscular. If we asked them to double-time during a march, they did. When we asked them to line up for inspection, they did. We didn't have any escapees and were blessed with only a few unruly soldiers – all of which were SS.

I was in Hallein for six weeks before headquarters transferred a company of MP's (Military Police) to my Detachment. It took two hundred twenty five MP's to do what we had been during our time there. We had done it very well, and I was awarded the Army Commendation Medal from Major General Harry Collins for my duty.

CHAPTER TWENTY-TWO

FIRE MARSHAL – UNITED STATES FORCES IN AUSTRIA
VIENNA, AUSTRIA
MAY, 1946

Once again, I found out that I was not able to make the grade to return home to the US. In spite of the high number of points I had accumulated, as an officer, I would have to stay for an additional two months. By this time, home was becoming more of an obsession. It had been over twenty months since I had seen my parents and my return home couldn't come soon enough. As homesick as I was, it was short-lived when I received an assignment to be the Fire Marshall of the USFA and was transferred to Vienna Headquarters. Getting back to the "City of Wine" and the friends I had made there was an ideal assignment for me, particularly on finding that I was able to keep my jeep driver, Nonamaker, and had an office with a secretary.

At the briefing for my new assignment, I was told that my requirements would be minimal since the position wasn't considered top priority. There had never been a major fire in the military facilities in Austria, and I was only required to give out monthly reports - and as the major said, "…no need to rock the boat" by trying to be innovative. With this being said, I was perfectly content to pass the remainder of my time in one of my favorite cities.

I tried to justify my position by making inspections of installations from a safety point of view - being hesitant to make any earth-shattering recommendations. I also developed manuals intended to place fire protection at an equal level in all of the installations. For some reason these efforts along with my inspection reports were received rather coolly by the USFA. Apparently they never put any weight in this position and didn't want any type of improvements or paperwork to stir up resentment with the Austrians.

In the meantime, I recognized that my time in Vienna was short, and I was lucky enough to have the friends I had made on my earlier assignment. I quickly reunited with Herr Sass and Herr Tempe and their families and again shared with them the food I had access to from the mess hall. We shared wonderful meals accented with stories of what had transpired since last I was with them, and we took up our friendship from where we left off. We also enjoyed the operas, concerts and ballets which through the occupation had been brought back into full brilliance.

As we became better acquainted, Herr Tempe offered me an engineering position on the Danube River Authority which had extensive plans for building numerous hydroelectric dams along the course of the river. I had every intention of taking him up on it – going back to Vienna after I finished my education. But, a little Rule lady changed my mind. (More about that later!) That spring in Vienna was a wonderful time for me and the fire safety program was nothing less than serene. It was just a matter of waiting for my time to be shipped out.

This wonderful and peaceful time wasn't to last! On May 16, 1946 in a UNERA (United Nations Emergency Relief Agency) dump site, a storage area for all types of equipment, clothing, food and material near Hallein caught on fire. The blaze happened when an improvised stove for heating a maintenance garage exploded. The fire spread over the fifteen acre storage area in a matter of minutes. We had little ability or access to equipment to put it out, or even control it.

The flames were so hot the equipment and materials melted as fifty five gallon drums of cooking oil exploded, shooting as much as three hundred feet in the air like a sky rocket! It was the most spectacular fire Austria had ever had in its history!

Hundreds of civilians ran to the storage area to help as best they could. It was heartbreaking to see them put their lives on the line to save whatever food they could salvage or get their hands on. The adjacent POW camp at Hallein, full of SS and other high risk German soldiers, was let out to help in our efforts. The officers took charge and organized the prisoners into teams to fight the hellhole - mostly with their hands, a few buckets, and an inadequate water supply. Additional aid from the Air Force fire fighters and equipment were flown from as far away as London and Rome. Bombers dropped water on the area but it all seemed to feed the flames. The loss was staggering for the times, estimated at $2-3 million dollars in monetary value – incalculable in what relief it could have given to the ongoing human suffering. It took over ten days and nights to put the fire out – it was never brought under control. Interesting enough, every prisoner returned to the POW camp; a miracle in itself when they could have escaped easily with the chaos they had just witnessed.

So much for the serenity of my life as a Fire Marshall in Austria. In the course of events, generals came from SHAFE to investigate and produced reams and reams of reports. In the confusion of the whole matter, I became a minor player at the onset. And, with the mounting activity, I could see that the post I was to occupy only temporarily could now be the source of a life-long occupation making investigations and filling out reports. The complexity of the situation was overwhelming. But alas, the saints were with me! A lieutenant colonel was assigned to replace me in time for me to make a June 2nd ship home. General Harry Collins, USFA commander and former Rainbow commander, had a lot of fun with me and my position as being the Fire Marshal during the worst fire in Austria's history, suggesting I should always stay away from matches. But at the same time, Collins told me: "go on home". It was as sweet an order as I could ever have. Never had I carried out an order as enthusiastically as this one.

PART VI: GOING HOME

CHAPTER TWENTY-THREE

THE FINAL GOODBYE
JUNE, 1946

At a time when confusion was it its peak, when there was a need for some orderly leadership in conducting the business of unraveling the UNERA Dump Fire catastrophe, I received orders allowing me to go home as scheduled. Ever since the fire, the sense of doom had come over me. I knew that with all the massive numbers of investigations, extensive cleanups, and the process of reequipping the UNERA facility ahead of me I would now have to stay a year or more to clean up all the details. It was an all-consuming thought. So when my orders came through and General Collins said I could go home, I couldn't believe it. I quickly set out to organize most of the details and paperwork and handed the job over to my replacement. It didn't take me long to gather my personal belongings and join another group of officers in Vienna who were also going home.

On June 2, 1946, we went by train from Vienna, Austria to Bremerhaven, Germany to the port of disembarkation for the USA. The ten hour rail trip was a nice one, particularly in comparison to the forty and eight boxcar excursions that had been our previous railcar experiences. It hadn't been that long ago when we had all been packed in boxcars crossing the country to our next front-line destination. Now we were scattered in a luxurious drawing room with tables set up where we played poker and other card games. To my surprise there were three Aggies on my train, also officers on their way home, who had been classmates of mine at the time the war broke out. We spent hours telling our experiences from the front lines and talking about our hopes for when we arrived home. The time flew by.

When we arrived at Bremerhaven there was an enormous, two-story, red-brick military installation filled with administrative offices that we shuffled through to fill out massive amounts of paperwork. We were assigned to barracks where we would wait for bureaucracy to finish its process and then wait again for our ship to depart. This time, the days dragged on. As additional Aggies filed in to do their form-filling, we enjoyed even more camaraderie, but a cloud of anxiousness kept us on edge. One night, we gathered outside our quarters with all the massive amounts of worthless script we had accumulated during our months of occupation, and threw them into an empty barrel and set it on fire. At first we were animated and talkative, but as the fire died down, we all grew silent as we watched the embers glow.

Finally, after six days of monotony, we received news that it was once again time to gather our personal belongings, but this time, it was to make the trip to the harbor to board our ship for home. Prior to packing our possessions, we were given military orders with a list of those items which were restricted to carry back to the States. Should I dare say "souvenirs"? The orders' intent was to insure that soldiers weren't taking any artifacts or collectables away from their homeland. Most of the soldiers felt the list of items was overly restricted and limited us from what we had previously known as acceptable pieces to take home. I was no exception. We carefully stashed those items in our bag that we really wanted and thought prudent in getting away with. The most that could happen would be to have the contraband confiscated, so the reward was worth the risk.

Admittedly, I was shaky as I walked up the gangplank to our ship home, carrying two duffel bags and a field bag full of loot. I had the German luger which the German officer had given me, other pistols, field glasses, cameras, etc. which I was sure would be on the restricted list and would be confiscated. Just in front of me, an A&M classmate was also clearly loaded to the gills with "souvenirs". As he was walking between the dock and the ship, while over the water, he eased each of his bags over the railing of the gangplank, dropping them into the harbor. Everyone had known that this particular soldier had confiscated some valuable souvenirs and were shocked that he had so easily forsaken them. But, he just smiled and told me he'd explain someday. I continued on as did the other officers and was lucky that none of my mementoes were confiscated.

The voyage to New York was markedly different from that of the trip from New York to Marseilles. We were quartered in comfortable and spacious staterooms, and our meals were served in the ship's dining room. Movies were all we had for entertainment on the ship, but the meals were good – at least those that I was able to keep down with my ever-present seasickness. This time, however, the seasickness was more bearable than during the boat ride to Marseilles. Looking back, I wonder if it was because my accommodations were so much more comfortable. We all found plenty of sack time where we gathered to visit and compare our plans. The main point of conversation was, that although we were going home, we were really going back to our schools to finish our education. After all, it was our goal and we didn't want to deny ourselves of an education. Our thoughts went on as to how we should handle our new assignment. Should we take up where we left off? Should we review the courses we had taken prior to being shipped out? Girls, too, were a major topic. Most of us had a special someone waiting for us at home, or at least we all hoped that she would be waiting for us, and we hoped to renew that relationship as soon as possible. Had they waited for us?

On June 18th, our ship sailed comfortably along until a marvelous woman could be viewed on the horizon – the Statue of Liberty. There is no grander sight for a returning soldier than this moment. Emotion on emotion surfaced when "the Lady" began to appear as just a speck, then slowly grew to a massive figure of freedom and love of country. Most of us had been cheated of bidding her farewell when we embarked that fateful day in November 1944 when we left under the cloak of darkness. So now, we marveled at how beautifully green she was. It was a surprise to many who hadn't known that she was made of copper. Almost everyone was on deck from the moment she appeared on the horizon until the ship passed the magnificent statue. We all saluted her and many were overwhelmed with tears as the ship gave a welcoming whistle - a shout-out that we were indeed back in the United States of America!

"New York, New York, a hell-of-a-town!"

Hot! That day in June, 1946 had to have set a record heat for the city. We were still dressed in the woolen shirts and trousers for the cold and sometimes frigid weather of Europe. But as we stepped out and into the sweltering heat most of us started to shed our clothes down to our much cooler long johns. A few of the men had khaki pants in their bags and quickly sold them for outrageous prices, only to don their woolens and suffer with the rest of us. The familiar hurry-up-and-wait of Army routines started up again until finally we were taken ashore by groups, with each group destined for different Army installations near our homes.

Although we pledged to come back after the war, we never made it back to New York City or the Commodore Hotel or the Club Zanzibar. We managed to get in a few "H-U-A-W" ("Hurry Up and Wait") times while we waded through debriefings and indoctrinations at Fort Dix in New Jersey, but the lights of home called us and we were eager to get there.

From Fort Dix I sent a telegram to my parents: "Ma, water down the soup. Your son's coming home!"

EPILOGUE

It was Friday, June 22, 1946 at Fort Sam Houston in San Antonio, Texas, a seemingly insignificant day at the time but looming much larger in years to come. The troop train arrived at the center, and we were assigned to quarters for the two to four day process of being discharged. San Antonio had no charm for the about-to-be civilians; we only wanted to get this over with! But the days drug on as we attended endless sessions on insurance, veterans benefits, educational benefits, medical information, indoctrination of civilian life, reserve service, and many other subjects that were important for our return to civilian life. We attended each session stoically, and made sure that our attendance was recorded. Saturday morning as I was being reviewed for release, it was pointed out that I hadn't attended the Reserve Service informational presentation. How could I have missed this? I had assumed it wasn't a necessary session because I didn't intend to move into the reserves. No excuses! I was told that I couldn't be released until Monday when I would be credited with having attended the presentation. On learning that if I signed up for the reserve, I would be allowed to go home that afternoon, I hurriedly signed up.... for which I would later have regrets. Big regrets. In short order, I had my discharge orders and suddenly the Army became strange and foreign to me. I resented the pomp and circumstance of Fort Sam Houston, and I saw it as something I had my fill of. I was fed up! I became angry and was spurred on to get on that bus headed for Rule, Texas.

The trip home to Rule from San Antonio seemed to crawl at a snail's pace. The bus stopped at every town, with pauses seeming interminable. Austin, Lampasas, Brownwood, Abilene and all points in between. Although the country was dry, barren, desolate, thinly populated and completely unlike what I had become used to in Europe, it still looked like the land of milk and honey to me. This was where my heart was. This was where Rule was. This was where Mother and Dad and Jiggs were. My home. The bus arrived in Haskell late in the afternoon. I looked for a ride to Rule and instead called my folks. Having no idea when I would arrive, they were shocked and elated and immediately drove the ten miles to the Haskell bus stop. There I stood with my two bags and a grin from ear to ear. No words can ever express the depth of feelings that I had as I drove into Rule, saw the familiar homes lining the highway coming into Rule, and seeing my uncle's grocery store. Then, I saw my Dad's drug store on the right. It was exactly where I had dreamed of it. On its door was a handwritten sign swinging from the door – CLOSED! GOING TO PICK UP MY SON!

And look! There's the bank, the filling station, the Cole House Bed and Breakfast, the Smith home. Suddenly it was too much for me and I began to cry like a baby. Home.

A lot of newspapers wrote articles about the difficulties for servicemen coming home and the government published instructions to help families rejoin and normalize. Those difficulties had entered my mind as well. Would I have sleepless nights? Nightmares? Would I be moody and try to disassociate myself from everyone? What would my parents expect for my readjustment? The first night I arrived, I ran across the street to see my girlfriend, Helen Ruth Cloud. After a warm welcome and hours of talk, I went home and slept for about eighteen hours. The next few days I spent visiting around town and seeing the many friends and neighbors who had been in my thoughts while I was away.

And next stop? Back to A&M to finish where I had left off.

Normalcy? I'm not sure I would ever be normal again…?

AFTERWORD

Dad lived the rest of his life happily surrounded with family that loved him. He finished school at A&M with a degree in Engineering and married his longtime sweetheart, Helen "Skipper" Cloud, the girl next door. He had three daughters and six grandchildren. He stayed active in all things "war". He wrote on the Civil War, and yes, after a conversation with me, he wrote on his activities in WWII. When all people commensurate on their lives or their loved ones lifetime, it's wonderful to be able to say… "and it was good." Dad's life was good.

Now to answer a few questions you may have on your mind. Some of the names have been changed in the book to protect the soldier's reputation. For instance, in Chapter 4, Dad described "one of the flashier soldiers" who was believed a coward. The name, Albert Ackermann, is a fictitious name given to the individual who was held in low esteem. Another name, Private Chapiro, from Chapter 8, was the older soldier with eleven children and one eye, who was drafted at thirty nine years. His age and afflictions wouldn't allow him to be an effective soldier. Although his crying and frightened conduct unnerved his fellow comrades, I was touched by the way the other soldiers tried to help him through his ordeal. Nevertheless, I felt this was another name that best be changed.

My dad's account of Dachau was from the perspective of having arrived separately from elements of his unit. If you recall, he was infirmed from his wound right up until the days prior to the liberation of the camp, and had been away from any of the major activity of his unit. Nevertheless, he undoubtedly knew much of the situation, not just from his personal observations when he arrived, but from later hearing the stories from the other men of his unit. They were some of the first soldiers who had marched into the camp. I've read many WWII books since writing about Dad's experiences at Dachau. There are hundreds of thorough accounts and books dedicated solely to the liberation. Interestingly, they all differ in minor details regarding who and when the camp was entered, the happenings of the Germans in the lookout towers, and other activities of the camp. Bear in mind that Dad wrote of his experience, and it's not meant to discard any other soldier's account. It was his personal experience.

One major question surrounds the prisoner from Dachau that was found alive among the stack of bodies on a box car in Chapter 13 The prisoner #64923 was a Pole named Gleb Rahr. He became famously known as the POW that defied death. He went on to make presentations on Dachau and gave speeches across the country. In 1994 he visited a Rainbow Veterans reunion where he was given the opportunity to personally thank his liberators.

In recent years there has been inconclusive research that may bring another survivor of the death train to light: Abraham Feffer. My feeling while compiling Dad's memoirs is that it matters not which of these men were rescued – it is wonderful to know and acknowledge yet another survivor of the horrors.

In Chapter 19, you read about the Sass family of which my dad was particularly close. He corresponded with them regularly for a few years after the war. His last letter was from Mama Sass in February 1949, when she gave my dad the news that Papa Sass had passed away from a heart attack. I can only imagine my dad's distress after hearing the news. He loved the family and often spoke about them during our talks around the dinner table. Additionally he corresponded with Eduard Tampe, Papa Sass' friend in Vienna. They were newsy letters and always managed to talk about the skiing that Dad liked so much.

And finally, what in the world happened at the port in Bremerhaven when his Aggie classmate eased his bags over the gangplank, dropping it into the harbor, and what was he hiding? Dad told us of a visit he made to his classmate's home. Here, his fellow soldier took Dad to his room, opened his sock drawer, pulled out a pouch, and with a dramatic swoop dumped the contents on his bed cover showing several hundred precious cut stones! The fellow explained that after dumping his bags in the harbor, he crossed the gang plank and somehow was able to fish them out, allowing him to successfully pass the ship officer's search. By the way, this was another name best not mentioned!

All in all, Dad served in WWII for forty six months and came out of it with shrapnel floating around in his chest cavity and memories that haunted him for the rest of his life. I'm grateful he wrote those memories down, and yes, I can say his life was extraordinary because of those.

I hope you enjoyed his account.

Celia Westbrook Thrash

ACKNOWLEDGEMENTS

As the saying goes "It takes a village…" And this book is no exception. Thank you to my dad for his service and for keeping the piles of information, letters, diaries, and photos of his experiences; there wouldn't be a "Baker Catcher" without him. There are lots of hugs to give to my sisters for their encouragement and memories they shared in this book, as well as to my friends Erin and Zac for their support, wisdom, and diligent work. They took on my project as if my dad was their dad, and helped bring life to his adventures. Thank you.

    Celia Westbrook Thrash

Made in the USA
Monee, IL
23 June 2023